Proceedings of the Orphan's Court

Washington County District of Columbia

1801–1808

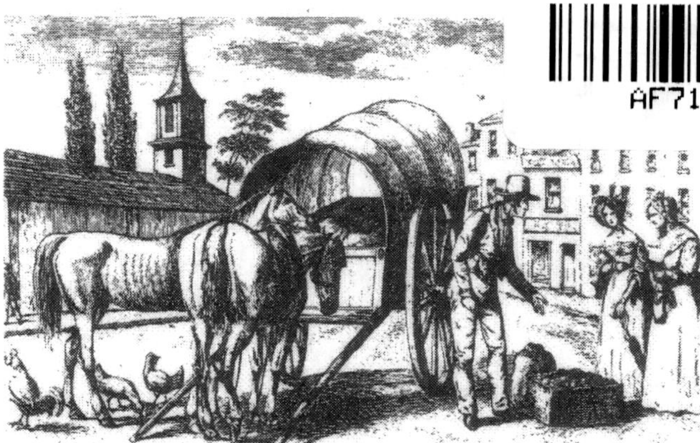

Wesley E. Pippenger

HERITAGE BOOKS
2015

HERITAGE BOOKS
AN IMPRINT OF HERITAGE BOOKS, INC.

Books, CDs, and more—Worldwide

For our listing of thousands of titles see our website
at
www.HeritageBooks.com

Published 2015 by
HERITAGE BOOKS, INC.
Publishing Division
5810 Ruatan Street
Berwyn Heights, Md. 20740

International Standard Book Numbers
Paperbound: 978-1-888265-65-1
Clothbound: 978-0-7884-6244-3

INTRODUCTION

The Orphans' Court of the District of Columbia, as constituted by law in 1801, continued until 1870, when its functions were transferred to one of the Justices of the Supreme Court of the District of Columbia holding a special term for probate business. The Register of Wills is also the Clerk of the Probate Court. William Hammond Dorsey, who had been active for some time in a number of prestigious positions, was appointed the first Judge of the Orphans' Court of Washington County, and at the same time, John Peter, was appointed Register of Wills. Although Peter was appointed to this position by President Adams, he did not serve in the capacity, for the record documents John Hewitt, an attorney, as the Register during this period. William Hammond Dorsey was succeeded as Judge of the Orphans' Court by Robert Brent. Brent, who was the first Mayor of the city, and who would later be paymaster-general of the army, served as Judge until 1814.

The clerk's office for Washington County was located during the first few months in a house on the south side of F Street and presumably at the southeast corner of 15th and F Streets, or just east of the corner. On the second Tuesday of April, 1801, the Orphans' Court convened in the house of William Rhodes, a tavern at the northeast corner of 15th and F Streets.[1] Some of the activities found in the proceedings presented in this work can be confirmed by related announcements that appeared in the local newspapers: *National Intelligencer*, *Washington Federalist*, or the *Georgetown Museum*.

Several separate journals, which now can be found at the District of Columbia Archives, make up a series of minutes for the Orphans' Court of the City and County of Washington, District of Columbia. The journals are presented here as full transcripts, with spelling, capitalization and punctuation preserved. The individual items cover the following years:

1. April 14, 1801 to February 9, 1802, uninscribed. A loose table of contents sheet indicates the original journal contained at least 20 pages.
2. October 11, 1803 to April 10, 1804, inscribed "Rough Minutes of Proceedings of The Orphans' Court, Washington County, Columbia — 11th Octo. 1803"
3. April 10, 1804 to April 8, 1806, inscribed "Minutes of The Proceedings of The Orphans' Court of Washington County, Columbia, Commencing 10th April 1804"
4. April 29, 1806 to September 10, 1808, inscribed "Minutes of the Proceedings of the Orphans' Court of Washington County, Commencing the 29th of April 1806, ending 10 September 1808, Washington City"

Of particular interest in these proceedings is the recording of over 80 apprenticeship records that are not found among the regular bound books of apprenticeship indenture

---

1. F. Regis Noel and Margaret Brent Downing, The Courthouse of the District of Columbia (Washington, D.C.: Judd & Detweiler, Inc., 1919), pp. 39, 41; Wilhelmus Bogart Bryan, A History of the National Capital: From its Founding Through the Period of the Adoption of the Organic Act, 2 vols. (New York: The MacMillan Co., 1914), Vol. I, p. 414. Additional information about the early government structure of the District of Columbia can be found in either of these sources, or William Tindall, Origin and Government of the District of Columbia (Washington, D.C.: Government Printing Office, 1909).

records. These books were recently abstracted by former D.C. archivist Dorothy S. Provine.[2] Also noteworthy in this series is the recording of certifications for Judge William Hammond Dorsey, Register John Hewitt, and several attorneys accepted for practice in the Orphans' Court.

Genealogists will find useful information for constructing the sequence of events involved in settling estates of deceased persons — some cases continue for many years. The minutes show connections of seamen with particular branches of the military and specific vessels; or even birth dates, residences or assigned trades that are customarily documented in apprenticeship indentures.

Wesley E. Pippenger
Arlington, Virginia
1998

2. Dorothy S. Provine, District of Columbia Indentures of Apprenticeship, 1801-1893 (Lovettsville, Va.: Willow Bend Books, 1998). The introduction in this work contains useful background information about the District of Columbia court structure and the use of apprenticeship indentures.

UNTITLED BOOKLET
ORPHANS COURT[3]
April 14, 1801 to February 9, 1802

[page 1]
At a session of the Orphans' Court for the County of Washington in the District of Columbia begun and holden at the house of William Rhodes on the 14th day being the second Tuesday of April in the year 1801, were present:

William Hammond Dorsey, Esquire, Judge
John Hewitt, Register of Wills for said county

The said William H. Dorsey having produced his commission and certificate of qualification as Judge — Ordered the same to be entered on the proceedings of the Court — and they are accordingly entered as follow to wit: Thomas Jefferson President of the United States of America, To all who shall see these presents Greeting, Know ye That whereas on the 3d day of this present month of March the Senate of the United States, did on the nomination of the President of the United States advice and consent that William Hammond Dorsey should be appointed Judge of the Orphans Court for the County of Washington in the District of Columbia. Therefore be it known That reposing especial Trust and confidence in the Wisdom, uprightedness and learning of him the said William Hammond Dorsey, & in pursuance of the advice and consent aforesaid, and do authorize and empower him to execute and fulfil the duties of that office according to the constitution and Laws of the United States, and To Have and To Hold the said office, with all the powers, privileges and emoluments to the same of right appertaining to him the said William Hammond Dorsey during his good behaviour. In Testimony whereof I have caused these Letters to be made patent and the Seal of the United States to be hereunto affixed Given under my hand, at the City of Washington the twenty sixth day of March in the year of our Lord one thousand eight hundred and one, and of the Independence of the United States of America the twenty fifth.

[seal] By the President Th: Jefferson.
Levi Lincoln, acting as secretary of State

[page 2]
District of Columbia County of Washington to wit. William Hammond Dorsey appeared before me this 14th day of April 1801 — produced his Commission as Judge of the Orphans' Court for the County of Washington and took and subscribed the oath to support the constitution of the United States as by the act of Congress prescribed also the oath of office as prescribed by law — and also repeated and subscribed a declaration of his belief in the Christian Religion. Before me a Justice of the peace in and for the County of Washington.

Thomas G. Addison.

---

3. The booklet for this period contains unlined paper that measures 7-1/2" wide by 13" high. Pages are numbered from 1 to 16. A separate table of contents sheet contains entries up through page 20.

John Hewitt having produced his Commission as Register of Wills for the County of Washington and also his Certificate of his qualification as such ordered that the said Certificate be entered on the proceedings of this Court — and the same is entered accordingly as follows to wit; District of Columbia, Washington County, to wit: John Hewitt appeared before me the 14th day of April 1801 — produced his Commission as Register of Wills for the County of Washington and took and subscribed the oath to support the constitution of the United States and the oath of office as prescribed by law and also repeated and subscribed a declaration of his belief in the Christian Religion. Before me a Justice of the peace in and for the County of Washington.

Thomas G. Addison.

Ordered that the said Certificates of qualification be lodged with the Clerk of the Circuit Court of the United States of the District of Columbia for the County of Washington.

James Sewell Morsell Esquire having made application to be admitted an Attorney of this Court and having taken the Oath to support the constitution of the United States and the oath of office he is admitted accordingly.

Augustus B. Woodward Esquire having made application to be admitted as an attorney [page 3] of this Court and having taken the oath to support the Constitution of the United States and also the oath of office — he is admitted accordingly.

Alexander Young applies for Letters of administration *de bonis non* on the estate of William Young deceased — and also for Letters of administration on the estate of Ruth Ann Young deceased — Ordered that the same be Granted him at the expiration of seven days from this day on filing bond to be approved according to law.

The Court then adjourned until tomorrow morning 10 o'clock —

Wednesday 15th of April 1801

The Court met according to adjournment

Present: William H. Dorsey, Esquire, Judge
John Hewitt, Register

Stephen Joice an orphan child without any parent living of the age of fifteen years, being produced in Court and it appearing to the Court that the said Stephen Joyce is destitute of all means of support, The said Stephen Joyce is by the Court placed with and bound unto William Giberson of Washington County, Bricklayer until the age of twenty one years to be taught the trade of a Bricklayer. The said William Giberson, being present in Court agrees and contracts and binds himself that he will instruct or cause to be instructed the said Stephen Joyce in the said Trade of a bricklayer in the best manner he is able and that he will find and allow the said apprentice good and sufficient sustenance and cloathing during the term aforesaid and that he will during the time aforesaid give the said Stephen Joyce six months schooling to be instructed in reading, writing and arithmetic and in all other respects conform to the laws in [page 4] upon this subject made and provided —

The Court adjourns until Tuesday next 10 'clock.

Tuesday 21st April 1801

The Court met according to adjournment.

Present William H. Dorsey, Esq., Judge
John Hewitt, Register

George Washington Brown an orphan child without any parent living aged seventeen years the first day of August next, being produced in court and it appearing to the court that the said George W. Brown is destitute of the means of support the said George Washington Brown is by the Court placed out with and bound unto John Minchin of the City and County of Washington, Boot and Shoe-maker until the age of twenty one years, to be taught the Trade and mystery of a Boot maker and shoemaker, the said John Minchin being present here in Court agrees contracts and binds himself that he will instruct or cause to be instructed the said George Washington Brown in the said Trade of a Boot and shoe maker in the best manner he is able and that he will find and allow the said apprentice good and sufficient sustenance and cloathing during the time aforesaid — and in all other respects conform to the laws on this subject made and provided —

The Court then adjourned until the second Tuesday in June next.

Monday 18th of May 1801.

The Court met this day on the special application and request of Elias Boudinot Caldwell.

Present: William H. Dorsey, Esq., Judge
John Hewitt, Register

[page 5]

Elias Boudinot Caldwell produces to the Court an attested copy, under the seal of the Register of Wills of Montgomery County in Maryland of the last will and testament of Gustavus Scott late of Washington County in the District of Columbia deceased and of the authentication and probate thereof -- ordered that the same be recorded by the Register of this Court -- He also produces the following written renunciations of the right to the executorship and administration to the said Gustavus Scott's Estate, viz:

A Renunciation of the executorship by Uriah Forrest dated the 13th of April 1801.

A Renunciation of the executorship by Thomas J. Bullitt dated the 18th day of April 1801.

A Renunciation of the executorship by John Threlkeld dated the 15th of May 1801.

A Renunciation of the executorship by Nathaniel Cranford dated the 9th of May 1801.

A Renunciation of the right to administration by Margaret Scott and Eliza C. Scott dated the 9th of May 1801.

A renunciation of the right to administration by John C. Scott dated the 16th day of May 1801 -- and the said Eliza C. Scott, Margaret Scott and John C. Scott, respectively, request that administration may be granted to Elias B. Caldwell.

And the said Elias Boudinot Caldwell applies for letters of administration with the will of the said Gustavus Scott annexed and having Given Bond in the penalty of Fifty thousand dollars with Benjamin Stoddert and John Peter as securities and having taken the oath of office as by law prescribed -- Letters of administration with a copy of the will of the said Gustavus [page 6] Scott deceased thereto annexed are granted him by the Court.

On application of the said Caldwell -- a warrant was issued directed to Thomas Beall of George and Charles Wayman authorizing them to appraise the goods chattels and personal estate of the said deceased Gustavus Scott.

And then the Court adjourned until the second Tuesday in June next.

Tuesday June 9th 1801.

The Court met according to adjournment
Present: William H. Dorsey, Esquire, Judge
John Hewitt, Register

George Blagden one of the executors of the last will and testament of John Emery applies for letters Testamentary on his estate -- but it appearing to the Court that Samuel Emery the other executor therein named is absent -- and it being alledged that he is not a Citizen of the United States -- it is ordered that notice of this application be published in the *George Town Museum* and some one of the Baltimore news-papers, once a week for the space of six months that the said Samuel Emery may appear if he think fit and take upon himself the joint executorship first complying with the law in such cases -- and that until the expiration of the said six months no letters testamentary issue to the said George Blagden unless the said Samuel Emery appear. It is further Ordered that in the meantime Letters to Collect be issued and granted to the said George Blagden -- and he having given bond with William Levering and Thomas Jones as his securities in the penalty of six thousand dollars for the faithful performance of his duty and having taken [page 7] the oath of office as by law prescribed, Letters to Collect the Goods of the said John Emery are Granted to him accordingly.

On application of the said Blagden a warrant of appraisement is issued directed to Henry [Moore] and Henry Ingle ---

Robert Ware Peacock on application is admitted as an Attorney of this court having first taken and subscribed to several oaths of office.

And then the Court adjourned until Tuesday next.

Tuesday June 16th 1801.

The Court met according to adjournment
Present: William H. Dorsey, Esquire, Judge
John Hewitt, Register

Constantine Gormley [sic] applies for letters of administration on the estates of Owen Gorman and Jacob Pascall late of Washington County deceased -- Ordered by the Court that he give notice of his said application by advertisement once a week for the space of three weeks in the *George-Town Museum* and in one of the Baltimore newspapers and that letters be granted him unless cause to the contrary be shewn written that time —

Adjournment until second Tuesday in August next.

Tuesday 30th July 1801.

Court meets this day on the application and request of George Blagden —

Present: William H. Dorsey, Esquire, Judge
John Hewitt, Register

On application of George Blagden executor of John Emery it is ordered by the court that the said Blagden sell the negroes and all the other personal property of the said deceased John Emery contained in the Inventory [page 8] returned by him — at public sale — for the purpose of paying his just debts and legacies — and that the said George Blagden give three weeks notice of the time place and manner of sale in one of the Georgetown newspapers -- that where the sum bid does not exceed twenty dollars the sale be for ready money but if above twenty dollars bond with good security be taken for payment of the money with interest in six months from the date.

It is further Ordered and directed that the said Blagden give notice, in one of the George Town and one of the Baltimore newspapers once a week for one month, of his having obtained Letters Testamentary on and for the Creditors to exhibit their claims against the said estate.

And then the Court adjourned until the 2nd Tuesday in August.

Tuesday 10th August 1801.

Court meets this day. Present: William H. Dorsey, Esq., Judge
John Hewitt, Regr.

Mary Corcoran an orphan girl without any parents aged about thirteen years as nearly as can be ascertained, is produced in Court and it appearing to the Court that the said Mary Corcoran is needy and destitute of all means of support — she is put out and bound as an apprentice to David Ogilvie of the County of Washington until she comes to the age of sixteen years — which said Ogilvie being present here in court agrees and contracts, on his part, to maintain and support her in a comfortable manner and to teach and instruct her in the manner usual with female apprentices — he also engages to instruct her in reading —

Ordered that Letters of Administration issue to Andrew McDonald on the estate of James Lyle on his filing Bond with the Register [&] with security, to be him approved.

Adjourned until Friday next.

[page 9]

Friday 13th of August 1801.

The Court met according to adjournment --

Present: William H. Dorsey, Esq., Judge -- John Hewitt, Register

Adjourned until Tuesday the 25th August.

Tuesday 25th of August 1801.

Court met according to adjournment --

Present: William H. Dorsey, Esq., Judge
John Hewitt, Register

Solomon, an illegitimate free negro boy aged ten years the seventeenth day of May last is produced to the Court by his mother negro Rachael and with the consent of his said mother is bound as an apprentice to Patrick Curry of the City and County of Washington, Joiner to learn the said trade and art of a Joiner, until he arrives to the age of twenty one years — and the said Patrick Curry being present in Court consents to take the said negro boy as an apprentice and contracts and agrees on his part, to instruct the said Solomon in the trade and art of a Joiner and to find and provide him with good and sufficient meat, drink, cloathing, washing, and lodging — and also to instruct him in common reading and writing —

Ordered that as no person has pursuant to notice in the public papers, attended to contest his right to the same, Letters of administration on the estate of Owen Gorman late of the County of Washington deceased, issue to Constantine Gormley on his filing Bond with two Securities to be approved of by the Register of this Court as by law prescribed, with the Register —

Adjourned until the second Tuesday in September.

Tuesday 8th September 1801.

The Judge attended and adjourned until Tuesday the 22nd September --

Tuesday 22nd September 1801.

The Court meets according to adjournment.

Present: William H. Dorsey, Esquire, Judge
John Hewitt, Register

[Page 10]

Charles Dean an Orphan white child aged fifteen years the seventh day of the present month of September is produced in Court by his mother Mary Montgomery and is by the Court with the approbation and consent of his mother put and bound out as an apprentice unto Richard Parrott of the County of Washington, Ropemaker, until he arrives at the age of twenty one years, and the said Richard Parrott being present here in court consents and agrees to take the said Charles Dean as an apprentice and agrees and contracts, on his part, to learn and instruct the said Charles Dean in the art and trade of a Ropemaker to find and provide him with good and sufficient meat, drink, cloathing, washing and lodging until he comes to the age of twenty one years and also to have him instructed in common reading writing and arithmetic —

Felix Dean an Orphan white child aged thirteen years the first day of December next is produced in Court by his mother Mary Montgomery and is by the Court, with the approbation and consent of his said mother, put and bound out as an apprentice unto

Richard Parrott of the County of Washington, Ropemaker, until he arrives at the age of twenty one years, And the said Richard Parrott being present here in court consents and agrees to take the said Felix Dean as an apprentice and agrees and contracts, on his part, to learn and instruct the said Felix Dean in the art and trade of a Ropemaker to find and provide him with good and sufficient meat, drink, cloathing, washing and lodging until he comes to the age of twenty one years — and also to have him instructed in common reading writing and arithmetic —

[Page 11]

Ordered that Letters *ad colligendum* on the estate of Harper Orrow late of the County of Washington deceased, issue to Robert King senior on his filing bond with two securities & in such penalty as shall be approved by the Register of this Court.

On the application of Elias B. Caldwell administrator with the will annexed of Gustavus Scott deceased, Ordered by the Court, that the said Elias B. Caldwell sell to the highest bidder at public auction all the negroes and other personal property of the said Gustavus Scott contained in his inventory for the payment of his debts and that the Course of his proceeding be as follows: He shall give at least three weeks notice in some one of the George Town newspapers and also in some one newspaper published in the City of Washington and in one of the Alexandria and one of the Baltimore newspapers, of the time place and terms of sale — That where the property sold to any one purchased shall not exceed twenty dollars the same be sold for ready money, but where the property sold to any one purchaser shall amount to more than that sum — a credit of Six months be given the purchasers passing bond with good security for the payment thereof with interest from the day of sale —

Adjourned until the Second Tuesday in October next.

Tuesday [blank] October 1801.

The Court met. Present: William H. Dorsey, Esq., Judge -- John Hewitt, Register.

Adjourned until 31st instant.

Saturday 31st October 1801.

The Court met according to adjournment.

It appearing to the Court that Lewin Talburtt is the largest creditor of James Robinson deceased and he having applied for letters of administration on his estate Ordered that the same be Granted him [page 12] to the said Lewin Talburtt on his filing bond in such penalty and two securities to be approved by the Register of Wills for the faithful discharge of his duty — pursuant to law.

Adjourned until 7th of November.

Saturday 7th November 1801.

Court met.

Ordered by the Court that Lewin Talburtt administrator of James Robinson sell at public auction the whole of the personal property of the said Robinson as returned in the inventory by the said Talburtt as Collector and that he proceed as follows: — He shall give at least fifteen days notice in a Washington and in a George Town newspaper of the time, place and terms of sale — and where the property sold to any one purchaser shall be under twenty dollars — the sale be for ready money — but where it exceeds that sum a credit of six months from the day of sale be given — the purchasers giving bond with good security, for the payment of the money with interest from the day of sale, in six months.

Adjourned until the 2nd Tuesday in December next.

Tuesday 8th December 1801.

The Court met this day.

Present: William H. Dorsey, Esq., Judge
John Hewitt, Register

Robin Hood a poor boy who appears to be suffering from the indigence of his parents aged twelve years the twelfth day of April last is produced in Court — and is by the Court bound out and put as an apprentice to Andrew Thompson of the City of Washington [page 13] Joiner, until he arrives to the age of Twenty one years, to learn the said trade and art of a Joiner and to serve him during that time as an apprentice and the said Andrew Thompson being present in court agrees to take the said Robin Hood as an apprentice and agrees and contracts, on his part, to teach and instruct the said Robin Hood in the said art and trade of a Joiner, to furnish and provide him with meat, drink, washing, cloathing and lodging during the term aforesaid — and to have him instructed in common reading, writing and arithmetic and at the end of his apprenticeship to give and furnish him with a good suit of cloaths and a set of Bench tools worth, at least, five dollars.

George Rose, an orphan boy aged eighteen years the twentieth day of May last who appears to be destitute of the means of support is produced in court and is by the court put out and bound as an apprentice to George Craig of George Town, Stone Mason and bricklayer to serve the said George Craig as an apprentice to the said trade until he arrives to the age of twenty one years — and the said George Craig being present in Court agrees to take the said George Rose as an apprentice and agrees and contracts, on his part to teach and instruct the said George Rose in the trade and art of a stone mason and bricklayer, to furnish and provide [page 14] for him, during the said term, good and sufficient meat, drink, washing, cloathing and lodging, and to give him, at the end of his apprenticeship a good suit of common working cloathes.

Ordered that Andrew McDonald sell all the personal property of James Lyle deceased as contained in his inventory for ready money, for the payment of his debts -- and that he give ten days notice by advertisement in one of the Georgetown newspapers of the time, place and terms of sale and also by advertisement at the most public places in the City of Washington —

Adjourned until Tuesday next.

Tuesday 15th December 1801.

Court met according to adjournment.
Present: William H. Dorsey, Esq., Judge
John Hewitt, Register

Ordered that Lewin Talburtt administrator of James Robinson give notice to the creditors of the said James Robinson deceased to exhibit their claims to him, in the manner prescribed by law, by advertisement in the *National Intelligencer* of Washington City published for the space of four weeks —

Adjourned until the 2nd Tuesday in February next —

[Page 15]

Tuesday 9th of February 1802.

Court met. Present: William H. Dorsey, Esq., Judge
John Hewitt, Register

Ordered that a Citation issue against the following persons to shew cause why they have not returned Inventories — to wit

Samuel Llewellin administrator of Jacob Pascall

Catherine Campbell administratrix of Robert Campbell —

Martha Claget[t] administratrix of Walter Claget[t]

On application of Robert King collector of the estate of Harper Orrow the further time of Ten days is granted him to return an Inventory.

Ordered that Elizabeth DeCarnap and Henry Ingle administrators of Jasper DeCarnap Give notice in the form prescribed by Law in the Georgetown and Washington newspapers and one of the Baltimore Daily papers by advertisement inserted once a week for two months for creditors to bring in their claims —

Salisbury Carman a poor boy without any father aged seventeen years the 20th day of June next is produced in court by Joel Brown of the City of Washington, Hatter and is by the Court put out and bound as apprentice to the said Joel Brown to learn the Trade of a Hatter, until he arrives to the age of twenty one years — and to serve him as an apprentice during that time and the said Joel Brown being present in Court consents to take the said Salisbury Carman as an apprentice and agrees and contracts, on his part, to teach and instruct the said Salisbury Carman the Trade or art of a Hatter, to find and provide him good and sufficient meat, drink, cloathing [page 16] washing and lodging and to give him education in common reading, writing and arithmetic —

Ordered that Elias B. Caldwell administrator of Gustavus Scott — give notice by advertisement in a George Town, Washington City, Alexandria and Baltimore newspaper inserted once a week for two months — for Creditors to exhibit their claims against the estate of the said Scott.

[erased] Scott, one of the orphan children of Gustavus Scott deceased of the age of [blank] years, appeared before the Court — and the Court, at his nomination and at his request, appointed Elias Boudinot Caldwell his Guardian — of his property and estate.

Ordered that the said Caldwell give Bond, in the form prescribed by law, with two good securities to be approved of by this court and in the penalty of [blank] Dollars for the faithful performance of his duty as guardian — on or before the second Tuesday in April next —

[end of record]

ROUGH MINUTES OF PROCEEDINGS OF THE ORPHANS' COURT WASHINGTON COUNTY COLUMBIA October 11, 1803 to April 10, 1804 [4]

At an Orphans' Court holden on Tuesday the 11th of October 1803 at Rhodes' Tavern in the City of Washington were present:

William H. Dorsey, Esq., Judge
John Hewitt, Register

Ordered that Letters of administration on the estate of James Harrison late of Washington County deceased issue to Catherine Harrison and James Harrison they giving bond with approved security for the due execution of their office — The oath of office is administered to them.

Isaac Owens Executor of Samuel Williams appears and passes his first account.

Ordered that Elizabeth Wilson administratrix of Alexander Wilson give notice to Creditors of the deceased to exhibit their claims to her by advertisement in the usual form, inserted in a newspaper in the City of Washington once a week — three successive weeks.

Ordered that George Walker, executor of George Walker, give notice to Creditors to exhibit their claims against the said deceased by advertisement in the usual form inserted twice a week for three successive weeks in the Georgetown newspaper.

Ordered that Letters of Administration on the estate of William Lowry deceased issue to Caesar Lowry he having filed bond with approved securities, for the faithful discharge of the duties of his office and that the Register issue the same and administer the oath of office.

William Hamilton an orphan boy aged sixteen years the 22nd day of July last is brought into Court and is by the Court placed ad bound out as an Apprentice to James Green of the City and County of Washington, Bricklayer to serve him as an apprentice to the trade or art of a Bricklayer until he attain the age of twenty one years — and the said James Green, being present in Court, consents to take the said William Hamilton as his apprentice — and agrees and contracts on his part to teach or cause to be taught the said apprentice, William Hamilton, the trade or art of a Bricklayer, to find and provide for his said apprentice, during said term, sufficient and comfortable meat, drink, washing, cloathing and lodging, to have him instructed in common reading, writing and arithmetic as far as the rule of three inclusive and at the expiration of his apprenticeship, to give the said apprentice a good suit of Cloathes —

Nancy Adams, a black girl aged twelve years in March last, having no parents living, is produced in Court by her grandfather negro Joseph Adams — and is with the consent of her said Grandfather placed and bound out, by the Court, as an Apprentice to Thomas

4. The booklet for this period contains unlined paper that measures 6-1/2" wide by 8-1/2" high. It is not paginated. Writing appears on 19 of the 24 faces.

Hyde of Georgetown in the County of Washington until she attain the age of sixteen years to learn the business of House-wifery, to serve him as such apprentice until the age of 16 aforesaid — And the said Thomas Hyde, being present in Court agrees to take the said Nancy Adams as his apprentice — and to have her well and sufficiently taught and instructed in the said business of house-wifery — and that he will, during the term aforesaid, find and provide his said apprentice, good and sufficient meat, drink, washing, lodging and cloathing — cause her to be instructed in common reading and will give her a good suit of cloaths at the end of her apprenticeship.

Eliza Adams, a black girl aged six years the first day of August last, having no parents living, is produced in Court by her Grandfather negro Joseph Adams, and is with the consent of her said Grandfather, placed and bound out by the Court as an apprentice to Joseph English of Georgetown in Washington County, until she attain the age of sixteen years, to learn the business of Housewifery & to serve him as such apprentice until the age of sixteen years aforesaid — And the said Joseph English, being present in Court, agrees to take the said Eliza Adams as his apprentice, and to have her well and sufficiently taught and instructed in the said business of housewifery and that he will during the term aforesaid find and provide his said apprentice good and sufficient meat, drink, washing, lodging and cloathing — and well cause her to be instructed in common reading — and give her a good suit of cloathes at the end of her apprenticeship.

William Holly a mulatto boy, without parents living, aged thirteen years the first day of December next is brought into Court by his uncle negro Joseph Adams and is by the Consent of his said uncle, bound and placed by the Court as an Apprentice to Joseph Nevit of Washington County until the age of twenty one — to learn the business or art of a Planter and Farmer — and to serve him as such — And the said Joseph Nevit, being present in court agrees to take the said William Holly as his Apprentice and on his part, contracts and agrees to teach or cause to be instructed the said William Holly, during his said apprenticeship, the said business or art of a Planter and Farmer — to find and provide for him, during said term, good and sufficient meat, drink, cloathing, washing, lodging and other necessaries to have him taught reading and writing and at the end of his apprenticeship to give him a good suit of cloathes.

Edward Stone a free white boy without parents living, aged eighteen years the twentieth day of March next is produced in Court and, by the Court, is bound out and placed as an apprentice to Isaac Norris of Washington County — Cooper — to serve him until he attain the age of twenty one — to learn the trade or art of a Cooper — And the said Isaac Norris being present in Court on his part, agrees to take the said Edward Stone as an Apprentice asnd. contracts and engages to instruct and teach or cause to be taught and instructed the said Edward Stone — the business, art or trade of a Cooper — and during his said apprenticeship, to find and provide him good and sufficient meat, drink, washing, lodging, cloathing and other necessaries, to have him taught reading, writing and common arithmetic, and to give him, at the end of his apprenticeship, a good suit of cloathes —

Joseph Sparrow a boy aged twelve years the twelfth day of January next is brought into Court by his mother and with her consent is placed and bound out as an Apprentice to the Revd. Leonard Neale as President of George-Town College to serve until twenty one years of age and to learn the art or trade of a Taylor at said College and the said Leonard Neale being present in Court agrees to take the said Joseph Sparrow under his direction and agrees and undertakes to have the said Apprentice well and sufficiently taught and instructed in the said art or trade of a Taylor to have him provided and supplied with sufficient meat, drink, washing, cloathing, lodging and other necessities during said term, taught reading, writing and arithmetic and provided with a good suit of cloathes at the expiration thereof.

Betsy Shannon an orphan girl aged fourteen years the twenty fifth day of April next is produced in Court and is, by the Court placed with and bound out as an [Apprentice] to Honore Antoine Julien of the City and County of Washington, Cook and Confectioner, to serve him as such until she attain the age of sixteen years and to learn the art and business of a Cook and Confectioner — and the said Honore Antoine Julien being present in Court consents to take the said Betsy Shannon as his apprentice and agrees and contracts to teach and instruct the said Apprentice the said Art or business of a Cook or Confectioner and to find and furnish her with good and sufficient meat, drink, washing, cloathing, lodging and other necessities, during her apprenticeship, to have her taught reading, writing and arithmetic and, at the end of her apprenticeship, to give her a new suit of cloaths.

Agnes Cook administratrix of Charles Cook appears and passes her first account.

Court adjourns until Wednesday 26th inst.

Wednesday 26th October 1803

At a Session of the Orphans' Court on 26 Octo. 1803, Rhodes's
Present: Wm. H. Dorsey, Esquire, Judge — Jno. Hewitt, Regr.

Martha Clagett administratrix of Walter Clagett appears on her summons and passes her first account.

Andrew McDonald administrator of James Lyle appears and passes his third account.

Charles Whitley an orphan boy aged eighteen years the first of October 1803 is produced in Court and by the Court is placed and bound out as an apprentice to [Louis] Joseph Lihault and August Joseph Lihault of Georgetown in Washington County, Coopers to serve them as such apprentice until the age of twenty one — and to learn the art and trade of a Cooper — the said Lewis J. Lihault and August j. Lihault, being present in Court consent to take the said Charles Whitley as their apprentice and agree to teach him or cause him to be taught in a sufficient manner their said business, art or trade of Cooper, to find and provide him, during said term good and sufficient meat, drink, washing, cloathing, Lodging and other necessaries to have him instructed in reading, writing and arithmetic and at the end of his apprenticeship to furnish him with a good suit of Cloathes

David Reintzel and Joseph Mechlin — having filed bond with approved security for the faithful performance of their duty — ordered that Litters of Administration on the estate of Frederick Gucker late of Washington County deceased issue to them and that the Register administer the oath of office to them —

Ordered that Johanna Barry administratrix of Redmond Barry deceased give notice for the Creditors of the deceased to exhibit their claims by advertisement in the usual form inserted once a week four successive weeks in the *National Intelligencer* and that she sell the persl. property of the decd. or such part thereof as she may think proper at public auction — giving 15 d. notice of the time, place and terms of sale — by advert. in said paper inserted 3 times and by adverts. set up at the most public place in the City of W. & that for all sums above 20 dol. a credit of six mo. be given she taking bond with good security for payment with int. from the day of sale.

Adjourned.

At an Orphans' Court holden on Saturday the 29th day of October 1803 for the County of Washington were present: William H. Dorsey, Esq., Judge
John Hewitt, Register

Gustavus Hall Scott one of the Devisees of Gustavus Scott late of Washington County deceased appears in Court and being an Infant aged eighteen years the Second day of April next makes choice of Elias Boudinot Caldwell of said County as the Guardian of his person and property until the age of twenty one years — whereupon the said choice is approved by the Court and it is ordered that the said Elias B. Caldwell the appointed Guardian as aforesaid and that he give bond with security in the penalty of four thousand dollars, for the proper discharge of his duty as prescribed by law —

Adjd.

---

2 Novr. 1803.

Ordered that Orlando Cook administrator of Nathan Goodall deceased give Notice to the Creditors of the deceased to exhibit their claims against him by advertisement in the usual form inserted in a newspaper in the City of Washington twice a week for three successive weeks, Ordered also that the said administrator sell the personal property of the said deceased at public auction on a credit of sixty days where any purchaser shall buy to the amount of more than twenty dollars taking bonds with security for payment with interest from the day of sale — all sales under the above sum to be for Cash — but he shall give fifteen days previous notice of the time, place and terms of sale by advertisement in the *National Intelligencer* and at the most public places in the City of Washington.

22nd Novr. 1803

At a special Orphans' Court holden on Tuesday the 22nd Novr. 1803 —

Present: Will. H. Dorsey, Esq., Judge
Jno. Hewitt, Regr.

Sarah Crookshank and Charles Glover having made application for Letters of Administration on the estate of John Crookshank late of Washington County deceased and having given bond with approved security for the discharge of their duty — Letters of Administration are granted them — by the Court — Ordered that they give notice to Creditors of the deceased to exhibit their claims against him — by advertisement in the usual form inserted one month in a Geo: Town newspaper —

Adjd.

At an Orphans' Court holden on Tuesday the 13th of December for the County of Washington at Rhodes' Tavern in the City of Washington were present:

William H. Dorsey, Esq., Judge

John Hewitt, Register

Lewin Talburt[t], administrator of James Robinson appears and passes his third account. —

James Watson a poor boy aged seventeen years the first day of November last is produced in Court and is with the consent of his mother, placed and bound out by the Court as an Apprentice to William Thompson of George-town in Washington County, Coppersmith and Tin-plate-worker, to serve him as an apprentice to said Trade until the full age of twenty one years. The said William Thompson being present in Court, on his part consents to take the said James Watson as his apprentice and agrees and contracts to teach, or cause to be taught, the said James Watson his art, trade or mistery of a Copper-Smith and Tin-plate-worker during his apprenticeship, and that during said term, he the said William Thompson will well and sufficiently provide and furnish the said apprentice meat, drink, washing, cloathing, lodging and other necessaries and will cause him to be instructed in common reading, writing and arithmetic. —

Edward Crowley a poor orphan boy supposed to be nineteen years of age in June next is produced in Court and with his own consent is placed and bound out by the Court as an Apprentice to William Thompson of &c. (as in the former *mutatis mutandis*) —

Matilda Edmonston a poor orphan girl aged twelve years as nearly as can be ascertained is produced in Court by Thomas Handy Gilliss and is, with her own consent placed and bound out as an apprentice to the said Thomas H. Gilliss of the City and County of Washington to learn the business or art of a house-keeper and to serve him as such apprentice until she attains the full age of sixteen years. And the said Thomas H. Gilliss being present in Court agrees to take the said Matilda Edmonston as his apprentice and agrees and contracts to teach or cause to be taught the said apprentice the said business or art of a house-keeper and to find and provide her during said term sufficient meat, drink, washing, cloathing, lodging and other necessaries to have her instructed in common reading and writing and at the end of her apprenticeship to give her a new suit of cloathes.

Whitney having applied for Letters of administration on the estate of John Carter late of the Marine Corps in the City of Washington, deceased — Ordered that the same be granted to him on his giving bond with approved Security for the performance of his duty.

Adjd. to 15 Decr.

Thursday 15 Decr. 1803.

A[t] an Orphans' Court holden this day &c.

Present — Wm. H. Dorsey, Esq., Judge — Jno. Hewitt, Regr.

James D. Barry Admr. of Ellen Healy appears on Summons and returns an account of the personal property of the deceased.

Adjd.

Wednesday 28 December 1803

At an Orphans' Court — this day present

William H. Dorsey, Esq., Judge — Jno. Hewitt, Regr.

Margaret Turner a free black woman from Baltimore having applied for Letters of Administration on the estate of Richard Poleston a free black man deceased lately in the service of the United States a board the frigate *New York* as a seaman alledging that he was her son — and having produced to the Court sufficient evidence of her said relationship and of her freedom, by affidavits — Letters of Administration on the estate of said Richard Poleston Are Granted her — she having given bond with approved security for the faithful performance of the office — and the oath of office as prescribed by Law is administered to her —

Tuesday 10 January 1804

At an Orphan's Court &c.

Abijah Hunt of the Mississippi Territory applies for Letters of administration on the estate of John Cunningham a soldier late of the United States' army deceased claiming the same as a creditor — and having produced satisfactory evidence of his death and of his the said Hunt being a Creditor and also Given bond with approved security and taken the oath of office as by Law prescribed — Order that the Register issue said Letters at the end of seven days from this date —

Nicholas King of W. County having applied for Letters of administration on the estate of John Gantt late of Frederick County in Maryland deceased — and having shewn the assent of the administrator of said John Gantt in Frederick County aforesaid — that Letters should be Granted to the said Nicholas King in this County — and having filed bond with approved security for the due discharge of his duty. Ordered that Letters do Issue to him.

18th January 1804

Samuel Lane of Montgomery County in Maryland having heretofore applied to the register for Letters of administration on the estate of Hardage Lane late of said County deceased and having this day filed bond with approved security for the due discharge of his duty — Letters of Administration are this day granted him on some estate. The Oath of Office is administered to him.

14 February 1804

James McLaughlin having applied for Letters of Administration with the will annexed on the personal estate of Laurence Connelly late of the United States frigate *New York* seaman deceased — Ordered that he give notice of his said application by inserting a copy of this order once a week for three successive weeks in Smith's *National Intelligencer.*

Adjd. to Tuesday next.

Tuesday 21 Feby. 1804

Court meets, present Judge & Register

Benjamin Bacon one of the securities of Jane Burch admx. of Jesse Burch files a petition praying against her counter security (insert it) ordered that Summons issue thereon against said Jane returnable to Saturday next.

Saturday 25th Feby. 1804

Court meets &c.

Jane Burch appears on Summons ordered that she give Counter Security to Benjamin Bacon one of her securities before the 2nd Tuesday in April next —

Adjd.

Wednesday 14 March —

Court meets at request of Caesar Lowry, present &c.

Thomas Lowry having exhibited an account against the estate of William Lowry deceased — Ordered by the Court, with the consent of said Thomas Lowry and of Caesar Lowry the administrator that the said account with all other accounts and differences between the parties be referred to the arbitration of Thomas Turner and Anthony Reintzel and if they disagree with power to choose and umpire. [Registered]

Adjd.

Tuesday 10 April 1804 [page crossed through]

Court meets — Present: Wm. H. Dorsey, Esq.
John Hewitt, Regr.

Elizabeth Ireland applies for Letters of administration on the estate of her husband John Ireland late of Washington County deceased —

John O'Brien having applied for Letters of administration on the estate of John O'Brien late of Washington County decd. — and having filed the renunciation of the widows' decease and also Bond with approved security — Letters are this day issued to him.

Ordered that he give notice to Creditors of the deceased to exhibit their claims by advertisement in the usual form inserted once a week for four successive weeks in the *National Intelligencer*.

[end of record]

MINUTES
of
The Proceedings
of
The Orphans Court
of
Washington County
Columbia
April 10, 1804 to April 8, 1806 [5]

At an Orphans' Court holden on the second Tuesday being the 10th day of April 1804 at the City of Washington for the County of Washington were present:

William H. Dorsey Esquire, Judge
John Hewitt, Register

Elizabeth Ireland appears and applies for Letters of administration on the personal estate of her husband John Ireland late of Washington County deceased.

John O'Brien having heretofore applied for Letters of Administration on the personal estate of his brother James O'Brien late of Washington County deceased & having produced the renunciation of the widow of the decd. With a request and consent that the same be granted to him and also Bond with approved security for the due discharge of his duty — Letters are Granted to him.

Ordered that the said John O'Brien give notice to the Creditors of the deceased to exhibit their claims by advertisement in the usual form inserted once a week for four successive weeks in the *National Intelligencer*.

Rachael Masters administratrix of Richard Masters appeared on citation and returned an Inventory.

Martha Clagett administratrix of Walter Clagett appears on citation and passes her second account.

Elias B. Caldwell appears on Citation and passes his third account as administrator cum Testamente annexo of Gustavus Scott.

Ordered, on application, that Joseph Mechlin and Daniel Reintzel administrators of Frederick Gucker give notice of their administration and to Creditors of the deceased to exhibit their claims by advertisement in the usual form inserted three times in a Washington city paper.

The court adjourns until Wednesday the 18. of April.

5. The booklet for this period contains unlined paper that measures 7-3/4" wide by 6-1/2" high. It is not paginated and not all pages at the back are used.

Wednesday 18th April 1804

At an adjourned Orphans Court present Judge & Register.

James M. Lingan one of the executors of Richard Anderson appears on Citation and returns an inventory.

Joseph Parsons administrator of Samuel Munroe appears on Citation and returns an Inventory and List of Debts.

Robert Brent one of the Executors of Notley Young appears and for himself and other executors returns a List of Debts due his Testator and also passes his first account.

Jane Burch, having been summoned to answer the petition and complaint of Benjamin Bacon one of her securities in her administration bond as administratrix of Jesse Burch, appears and having produced the Bond of Kinsey Gittings as counter security to the said Benjamin Bacon— the same is deemed sufficient by the Court and ordered that she be discharged from further process under said petition.

Ordered that Jane Burch, administratrix of Jesse Burch give notice of her administration and to the Creditors of the deceased to exhibit their claims, by advertisement in the usual form inserted three times in a Washington City paper.

Caesar Lowry having appeared on Citation returns an Inventory of the goods and chattels of William Lowry deceased — the same being informal, further time is granted him to make such return and also time until the next court to return a list of debts.

The Court adjourned until Thursday 19th April.

Thursday 19. April.

David Waters one executor of James Seller appears on Citation and returns an account of personal estate — and as Executor of Andw. Rutherford makes affidavit that he knows of no personal estate.

Adjourn to 25th April.

Wednesday 25th April 1804

An adjourned Orphans' Court.

Sarah Fownes Executrix of John Fownes appears on Citation, returns a List of Debts due the deceased, of money received by her — and also passes her first account.

Samuel Smallwood having heretofore applied for Letters of administration on the personal estate of Richard Frazer late of Washington County deceased — and producing a written renunciation of Anna C. Frazer widow of the deceased and her consent and request that said Letters be issued to him — and having also entered into Bond with approved securities for the performance of his duty — Letters of administration on the personal estate of said Richard Frazer are Granted him.

Ordered that the same Samuel N. Smallwood give notice of his administration and for the Creditors of the deceased to exhibit their claims by advertisement in the usual form in the *National Intelligencer* and *Washington Federalist*.

Barbara Marshall having heretofore applied for Letters of Administration on the personal estate of her deceased husband John Marshal [sic] late of Washington County and having entered into bond with approved securities for the due discharge of her duty — Letters are Granted her.

The Court adjourns.

At a special Orphans' Court on Saturday 12 May 1804.

Ordered on application that Samuel N. Smallwood administrator of Richard Frazer deceased, for the purpose of paying debts, sell the personal property of the deceased contained in the Inventory returned by him — That the same be sold on the following terms: All purchases not exceeding twenty dollars — for cash: for all purchases above that sum on a credit of six months taking Bond with approved security for payment with interest from the day of sale. He shall also give at least twelve days previous notice of the time, place and terms of sale by advertisement, in a Washington City newspaper inserted three times and by advertisement set up at public places in the City of Washn.

Ordered that John O'Brien administrator of James O'Brien sell the personal property of the deceased contained in the Inventory &c. (On same terms in every respect as the above).

Court adjourns.

Wednesday 6th June 1804

[Registered]. A Special Orphans' Court.

Pontius D. Steele having heretofore applied for Letters of administration on the personal estate of David Valenzin late of Washington County deceased, and having entered into Bond with approved security for the due discharge of his duty, Letters are Granted him.

Adjourned.

At an Orphans' Court held on the second Tuesday being the 12th day of June, present:

William H. Dorsey, Esq, Judge
John Hewitt, Register

John Barnet a poor boy aged twelve years on the eleventh day of November next is brought into Court by his mother (having no father living) and is with his own and his mothers' consent bound by the Court to George Blagden of the City of Washington, Stone-Cutter to learn the art or trade of a stone cutter and to serve him as an apprentice until the age of twenty one years, and the said Blagden being present in Court agrees to take the said John Barnet as his apprentice and contracts on his part to teach or cause to be taught the said apprentice the art or trade of a stone-cutter during his apprenticeship, to find and provide him sufficient meal, drink, washing, lodging, apparel and other necessaries to teach or have him taught common reading, writing and arithmetic and at the end of his apprenticeship to furnish him with a good suit of cloathes.

Hannah Lockrey Gibbs an orphan girl aged fourteen years the thirteenth day of July next is brought into Court by Ezra Varden of the City of Washington, Taylor, and is placed & bound by the Court as an apprentice to the said Ezra Varden with her own consent, until she attain the age of sixteen years, to learn the art and business of House-wifery — And the said Ezra Varden being present in Court agrees to take the said Hannah L. Gibbs as his apprentice and contracts and agrees, on his part, to teach or cause to be taught the said apprentice the said art and business of House-wifery — and to find and provide for her during said apprenticeship, sufficient meal, drink, washing, lodging and other necessaries & to have her instructed in common reading, writing and arithmetic.

Theresa Kelly a poor girl whose parents appear unable to support her aged nine years the twenty fifth day of December next is brought into Court by her mother and is placed and bound by the Court, with her mothers' consent, as an apprentice to John C. Seiverman of the City of Washington, grocer, until she attains the full age of sixteen years — to learn the art or business of House-wifery — And the said John C. Seiverman being present in Court consents to take the said Theresa Kelly as his apprentice and, on his part, agrees and contracts to teach, or cause to be taught, the said apprentice the said art or business of House-wifery, to find her sufficient meat, drink, washing, cloathing and lodging and other necessaries — and to have her instructed in common reading, writing and arithmetic.

George Blagden, Executor of John Emery, appears and passes his final account.

Henry Ingle and Shadrach Davis administrators of Jasper DeCarnap appear and pass a second account.

Ordered That the Register issue Citations against all Executors or administrators who have failed to return inventories or list of debts or who have not regularly accounted with the Court for their proceedings.

Court adjourns.

Tuesday 14th August 1804

At an Orphans' Court this day, present:

William H. Dorsey, Esq., Judge
Jno. Hewitt, Regr.

Ordered that Margaret Winsett administratrix of John B. Winsett give notice to Creditors of the decd. To exhibit their claims, by advertise inserted in the National Intelligencer three times — Also that she sell the personal property of the deceased at public sale — giving two days previous notice thereof by advertisement set up at the most public places in the City of Washington — that the terms be that all persons purchasing to the amount of 20 dollars have credit of three months giving bond with security for payment with interest from day of sale, persons purchasing under that sum pay cash.

Agnes Cooke [sic] administratrix of Charles Cook appears on Citation and passes her second account.

Martha Clagett administratrix of Walter Clagett appears on Citation and now passes the final account of her administration by which it appears that there is a balance of personal estate of the deceased in her hands [amounts] to $1847 dollars & 78 Cents — and it appearing to the Court that the Intestate Walter Claget[t] died leaving six children.

Ordered that the said balance be distributed in manner following: one third to the said Martha Claget[t] as widow, the other two thirds among the said six children in equal portions. [Registered]

Archibald Bateman aged Ten years on the first day of April last a poor boy destitute of the means of support his father not residing in Washington County is brought into court by his mother and with her consent is placed and bound by the Court an apprentice to Louis Joseph Lihault of Georgetown said county Cooper to learn the said trade or art of a Cooper and to serve said Lihault as an apprentice to the said trade until he attain the full age of Twenty one years — And the said Louis H. Lihault [sic] being present in Court agrees to take said Archibald Bateman as his apprentice and to teach and instruct him the art or trade of a Cooper to find and provide for him, during said apprenticeship sufficient meat, drink, washing, cloathing, lodging and other necessaries and to have him taught common reading, writing and arithmetic.

William Burch a poor boy without parents and destitute of the means of support, aged Ten years the twelfth day of March last being produced into Court is bound, by the Court, an apprentice to Benjamin Fowler of George-Town, Cabinet-maker, to serve him as an apprentice in learning the said trade until he attain the full age of twenty one years, And the said Benjamin Fowler being present in Court agrees to take said William Burch as his apprentice and contracts and engages to teach him the said art and trade of a Cabinet-maker, to find and provide him during his apprenticeship, sufficient meat, drink, cloathing, washing, lodging and other necessaries and to have him taught common reading, writing, and arithmetic.

Adjd. To 1st Monday in Sept.

At an adjourned Orphans' Court holden for Washington County on Monday the 3rd day of September, 1804, were present:

William H. Dorsey, Esq., Judge
John Hewitt, Reg.

[blank] DeKrafft the widow of Charles DeKrafft late of Washington County deceas'd makes application for Letters of administration of his estate — he having died intestate.

Order for the administrators of James Harrison to sell the property of the deceas'd at public auction giving Ten days previous notice of the time, places and terms of sale, by advertisement in the Geo: Town newspaper that the said sale be on a Credit of six months to purchasers above Twenty dollars — [making] bond with security for payment with interest. Ordered also that they give notice by advertisement in the usual form inserted three times in a Geo. Town newspaper for creditors to exhibit their claims.

Charles Tomkins applies for Letters of administration on the estate of James Miller of Calcutta deceased.

Samuel Iams, a poor boy, having no father living, destitute of the means of support and aged twelve years the fifteenth day of October next is produced to the Court by his mother and is by the Court, with her consent, bound out and placed, as an Apprentice to Thomas Wannell, of the City and County of Washington, Boot and Shoemaker; to serve him, at said trade until he attain the full age of twenty one years. The said Thomas Wannell being present in Court agrees to take the said Samuel Iams as his appren. and contracts and agrees to instruct and teach or cause to be taught and instructed the said apprentice his said art or trade of a Boot and shoemaker and also that, during said apprenticeship, he will find and provide said apprentice sufficient meat, drink, washing, cloathing, lodging and other necessaries and will, further, have him taught common reading, writing and arithmetic.

The Court adjourns to the Court in course.

At a special meeting of the Orphan' Court holden October 4th 1804.

Present — William H. Dorsey, Esq., Judge
John Hewitt, Register

Martha Clagett is appointed Guardian to each of her infant children namely: — William Clagett, Mary Ann Clagett, Darius Clagett, Walter Clagett, and Martha Eleanor Clagett.

Ordered that she give bond in usual form.

James S. Morsell makes application for Letters of administration on the estate of Walter Mackall deceased.

Tuesday 9 October 1804

At an Orphans' Court holden the second Tuesday being the ninth day of October 1804, were present:

William H. Dorsey, Esq., Judge
John Hewitt, Register

Letters of administration of the personal estate of Daniel Develin deceased are Granted to Bernard Develin his brother — he having made application some time since and having this day filed bond with approved security for the discharge of his duty and taken the oath of office.

Ordered that he Give notice to creditors to exhibit their claims by advertisement in the usual form inserted once a week — four weeks in a Georgetown newspaper. [Registered]

Ordered, on application, that the Executors of Notley Young deceased sell so much and such further part of the negroes and other personal estate of the deceased — as they may deem necessary to discharge his debts — and that they sell the same on a credit of one half at four and the other half at six months taking bond with security for payment with interest from the day of sale — and that they give four weeks previous notice to such sale by advertisement in a Washington and Georgetown newspaper.

Ordered That William Cranch, Executor of Mary Williams deceased Give notice to the Creditors of the deceased to exhibit their claims against her — by advertisement in the usual form inserted once a week for four successive weeks in a City of Washington and a Philadelphia newspaper.

Ordered also that the said William Cranch sell so much of the personal estate of the deceased, for ready money, as may be sufficient to pay the debts, legacies, funeral expenses and his commission as Executor on the amount of the Inventory at the rate of seven and a half per cent.

Ordered that Letters of Administration, on the personal estate of James Deegins late of Washington County deceased, be issued to Nancy Deegins his widow on her filing bond with security to be approved by the Register in the penalty of five hundred dollars for the due discharge of her duty.

Orlando Cook having heretofore applied for Letters of Administration on the personal estate of Francis McClure late of Washington county deceased as a Creditor and established his claim to the satisfaction of the Court and filed Bond with approved securities — Letters are Issued to him.

Ordered that the said Orlando Cook give notice to Creditors to exhibit their claims against the said McClure decd. by advertisement in the usual form inserted in the *National Intelligencer* once a week for three successive weeks.

Sarah Fownes and [blank] having each applied for Letters of administration on the personal estate of James Thompson late of Washington County deceased, claiming the same as Creditors it was by mutual consent agreed That Letters of administration to said James Thompson should be issued by the Court to Henry Herford and Thomas Herty of said county jointly — they giving bond with satisfactory security for the faithful performance of their duty — and that on their so doing and at the expiration of twenty days from the death of the said Thompson letters issue to them.

Robert Duncanson; aged about fourteen years, an orphan, is produced in court by his uncle William M. Duncanson — and with his own and consent and consent of his uncle is placed and bound out as an apprentice to Peter Miller of the City and county of Washington, Baker — to serve him as apprentice to said trade for six years from the date hereof — And the said Peter Miller, being present in court, agrees and consents to take the said Robert Duncanson as his apprentice, for the term aforesaid — and contracts and agrees, on his part, that he will well and truly teach and instruct the said Robert Duncanson the art, trade and business of a Baker — that he will find and provide him sufficient meat, drink, cloathing, lodging and other necessaries during his apprenticeship and will also during said time, cause him to be well instructed in common reading, writing and arithmetic.

Court adjourned.

Tuesday 11. December (2nd Tuesday) 1804.

Court holden at Rhodes's Tavern

Present: Wm. H. Dorsey, Esq., Judge
Jno. Hewitt, Regr.

Patrick O'Brien an orphan boy aged sixteen years is brought into court by his uncle John O'Brien — and being destitute of the means of support and bound by the Court, with his own and uncle's consent as an apprentice to Ebenezer Nesmith of the City and county of Washington — house-carpenter and joiner, to serve him till the age of twenty one — at said trade — And the said Ebenezer Nesmith being present in Court, consents to take the said Patrick O'Brien as his apprentice and contracts and agrees to teach to said apprentice his said art or business of a House-carpenter and Joiner, & to find and provide him good and sufficient meat & drink, washing, cloathing, lodging & other necessaries — And further to cause him to be taught common reading, writing and arithmetic and at the end of his apprenticeship to give him a suit of cloathes with 15 Dollars.

John Hocker an orphan, of Washington County, aged nine years is brought into Court by his mother — and Daniel Reintzel of said County is, by the Court appointed Guardian to said John Hocker — Ordered that said Guardian give bond with securities for the faithful discharge of his duty, in the penalty of one thousand dollars.

Jasper M. Jackson, administrator of Margaret Magruder appears & Exhibits his account of her personal property.

Adjd.

Thursday 31st January 1805

At a special Orphans' Court at Rhode's [Tavern]

Trueman Burnes aged about fifteen years and Rebecca Burnes about twelve, infant children of James Burnes deceased are brought into Court and it appearing that they are entitled to Real-property within Washington County — The said Truman Burnes made choice of John P. Van Ness as his Guardian: — And the Court appointed said John P. Van Ness Guardian to said Rebecca Burnes — Ordered that said Guardian give bond, in each case — as required by law, in penalty of $1000.

Adjd.

Feby. 12, 2nd Tuesday 1805

At an Orphans' Court holden &c.: at Rhodes &c.

Present: William H. Dorsey, Esq., Judge
John Hewitt, Regr.

Aquila Proctor aged sixteen years on the first day of July next, a mulatto free boy destitute of the means of support is brought into court and is by the Court bound as an Apprentice to William Fields of Washington County - bricklayer and plaisterer to serve him to said trades until he attain the age of twenty one: The said William Fields being present in Court agrees to take the said Aquila Proctor as an Apprentice and contracts and engages to teach him the said trades or arts of a bricklayer & Plaisterer in a good and sufficient manner: to find and provide him sufficient meat & drink, cloathing, washing, lodging and other necessaries — and to have him instructed in common reading, writing and arithmetic.

Walter Proctor, aged fifteen years 1st August next as nearly as can be ascertained, a mulatto free boy destitute of the means of support, is brought into Court and is by the Court bound as an Apprentice to James [Patterson] of the City of Washington, Boot and Shoemaker — to serve him to said trade until he attain the age of twenty one: The said James [Patterson] being present in Court agrees to take the said Walter Proctor as his apprentice and contracts and engages to teach him the said trade or art of a Boot and Shoe maker in a good and sufficient manner: to find and provide him sufficient meat & drink, cloathing, washing, lodging and other necessaries and to have him instructed in common reading, writing and arithmetic.

Robert Collins aged seventeen years on the eleventh of the present month of February without father is brought into Court by his mother and with her and his own consent is bound as an Apprentice to John Glasgow of Washington County, Millwright and Miller — to serve him until the age of twenty one years. The said John Glasgow present in court agrees to take the said Robert Collins as his apprentice and contracts and engages to teach and instruct him so far as he can, the said trade and business of a Millwright and milling — to find him sufficient necessaries and comforts of life — and to have him instructed in common reading, writing and arithmetic.

On the application of the Executors of Francis Deakins Deakins [sic] decd. Ordered, That the said Executors give notice to Creditors of the decd. To Exhibit their claims, by Advertisement in the usual form inserted one month in the *National Intelligencer* and in the *Washington Federalist* and also three times in some one of the Baltimore paper —

On application of John Hoye administrator *de bonis non* of William Deakins decd., Ordered that the said Administrators give notice to creditors (in same manner as ordered above) —

Letters of Administration on the personal estate of Charles Laight late of the City and State of New York decd. — are Granted to John P. Van Ness of the City of Washington — he having filed his application in one time and entered into Bond as required by law.

Letters of Administration on the persl. est. of Willm. Laight late of New York decd. Granted to John P. Van Ness of the City of Washington, he having made application in one time and entered into Bond as is required by law.

Thomas Herty, on application, is admitted as an Attorney of this Court — having taken the Oaths of office &c.

Adjd.

Saturday 16 March 1805

On application of John N. Lovejoy, ordered That process issue from this court to being before the same negro Trese an orphan girl now in possession of Nicholas Fevrier & wife — for the purpose of binding her out.

Adjd.

Saturday 23rd March 1805

Negro Trese an orphan girl is persuant to the process of the Court issued on the 16th instant, brought into Court by the Marshall of the District of Columbia — and, being about thirteen years old, is bound an Apprentice to John N. Lovejoy of Washington County until the age of sixteen — to learn Housewifery — And the said John N. Lovejoy being present in court agrees to take the said orphan girl and to have her sufficiently instructed in the duties and business of Housewifery. That he will find and provide for her the necessaries and comforts of life and will have her taught common reading, writing & arithmetic, if capable.

Application having been made by Abner Cloud of Washington County for Letters of Administration on the personal estate of Nicholas Way late of the City of Philadelphia deceased. It is Ordered that the said Letters be ranted as prayed unless cause to the contrary be shewn to this Court on or before the 2nd Tuesday in June next and provided that a copy of this order be previously inserted at least twice a week between the 1st day of April and 1st of May next in any one of the Philadelphia newspapers.

Application having been made by Abner Cloud of Washington County for Letters of Admin. On the personal estate of Samuel Paxton late of Baltimore in Maryland deceased.

Ordered That the said Letters be granted as prayed, unless cause to the contrary be shew to this Court on or before the second Tuesday in June next provided that a Copy of this order be previously inserted at least twice a week, between the 1st of April and 1st of May next in some one of the Baltimore newspapers.

Application is made by Margaret Carlan widow of James Carlan late of Washington County deceased for Letters of administration on the estate of said deceased.

Richard Young an infant child of Abraham Young deceased, aged about twelve years is brought into Court and Charles Young his brother is appointed his Guardian.

Letters of administration are granted to Charles Young on the estate of John Young of Washington County, his brother.

Letters of collection are Granted to Alexander McCormick of Washington County on the personal estate of John Scott late of said county deceased.

Application is made at the same time by said McCormick for Letters of administration on said estate.

Application is made by John Bridges for Letters of administration on the estate or Christian [Slimmer].

Adjd. to Saturday next.

Saturday 30th March 1805

At an adjourned Orphans' Court.

On application of the President, Directors and Company of the Bank of Columbia — Ordered that summons issue against Elias B. Caldwell administrator of Gustavus Scott deceased to account for his administration of the personal estate of the deceased.

Adjourned until Saturday 6 Apr.

Saturday 6. April 1806

At an adjourned Orphans' Court &c.

Letters of administration are granted on the personal estate of James Carlan deceased to Margaret Carlan his widow.

Letters of administration are Granted to James Mathers Senr. of Washington County on the personal estate of James Mathers Jr. of said county his son. —

Adjourned till Tuesday next.

Tuesday (2nd in the month) 9 April 1805

At an Orphans' Court for Washington County

Present: William H. Dorsey, Esq., Judge
John Hewitt, Regr. Wills

There being no business Court adjourns until Saturday next.

Saturday 13th April 1805

At an adjourned Orphans' Court &c.

Present the Judge & Register

Ordered That the administrators of James Harrison give notice to Creditors to exhibit their claims against the deceased by advertisement inserted in the *Washington Federalist* once a week for three successive weeks.

Adjourned till Saturday the 27th of April

Saturday 27th April 1805

An adjourned Orphans' Court at Rhodes

Present: William H. Dorsey, Esq., Judge
John Hewitt, Register

Abednigo Ray a free boy aged seventeen years the 10th instant is brought into court and, by the consent of his father signified in writing, is bound and placed as an apprentice to Wilson Bryan of the City and County of Washington, Carpenter and Joiner to serve him to the age of twenty one years at said trade and the said Wilson Bryan being present in Court agrees to take the said Abednigo Ray as his apprentice and contracts to teach or cause him to be taught the said art and trade of a Carpenter and Joiner and during his apprenticeship to find and provide him with sufficient meat, drink, washing, lodging and other necessaries.

Letters of administration issued to John Coyle on the estate of John Woods he having given bond &c.&c.

Application is made by Kinsey [Gittings] one of the securities of James Burch administratrix of Jesse Burch for courts security. Ordered that Summons issue returnable on Saturday week.

4th May 1805

An adjourned Court

John O'Brien administrator of James O'Brien appears and passes his first account.

Adjd. to Saturday.

Saturday May 11th

An adjourned Orphans' Court

Kinsey Gittings applying for counter security from James Burch — ordered that Citation issue against her to shew cause — also to make her account.

Adjd.

Saturday 25 May 1805

At an adjourned Orphans' Court at Rhodes's

Present: Wm. H. Dorsey, Judge — Jno. Hewitt, Regr.

William Matthews a negro boy aged 8 years the 16th of September last, being the natural son of negro Rachael, is brought into court, and it appearing to the court that he is destitute of the means of support and that his parents are [incapable] of supporting him, he is bound and placed out by the court, with the assent of his mother who is personally present, to Henry Timms of the City and County of Washington, as an apprentice to learn the art and trade of a Joiner and House Carpenter — And the said Henry Timms, being present in Court agrees to take the said boy as his apprentice and engages to teach or cause him to be taught the art and trade aforesaid of a Joiner and house carpenter — to find and provide for him good and sufficient meat, drink, washing, cloathing, & lodging & other necessaries — and also, at the end of his apprenticeship to give him a new suit of cloaths worth 20 Dollars & a set of Bench tools for his trade and a suiter to teech him common reading and writing.

Charles Young administrator of John Young deceased, having this day returned an inventory of the personal estate of said deceased, in due form. Ordered on his application, that he sell the personal property contained in the inventory so returned, on a credit of six months, taking bond with security to be approved by this court, for payment with interest from the date — but he shall give three weeks previous notice of the time, terms and place of sale by advertisement in the *National Intelligencer* and set up at the most public places in the City of Washington.

Kinsey Gittings, one of the sureties of Jane Burch, having appeared, and the summons against her being returned non est — Ordered that said Summons be renewed, returnable to the 2nd Tuesday in June next.

Adjd. to Saturday next.

Saturday 1st June 1805

The Court meets — present: Wm. H. Dorsey, Esq., Judge
Jno. Hewitt, Regr.

Adjourns till Tuesday next.

Tuesday June 11th 1805 (2 Tuesday)

At an Orphans' Court for Washington County were present:

William H. Dorsey, Esq., Judge
John Hewitt, Regr.

Ordered that the Executors of Francis Deakins deceased sell at public auction, such part of the personal estate of the deceased as they may deem proper on a credit of six months to all purchasers above twenty dollars taking bond with good security for payment with interest — all sales under that sum to be for cash. But notice of such sale shall be previously given in the George-town and Washington newspapers at least twice a week for two weeks.

Ordered by consent of parties that all matters and accounts in controversy between the estates of William Deakins and of Charles Beatty deceased, be referred to the arbitration of Philip B. Key and James S. Morsell with power for them, on a difference of opinion to choose an umpire.

A caveat and petition signed John Way were exhibited, shewing reasons why letters of administration on the estate of Nicholas Way should not be granted as prayed by Abner Cloud — ordered that the same be filed.

The property of Jesse Burch ordered to be deliv'd. to security Gittings.

Adjourned until Saturday next.

Saturday 15 June 1805

At an adjourned Orphans' Court — present the Judge and Register.

Isaac Owings Executor of Samuel Williams appears in Court and shewing that there are suits depending relative to the estate of the deceased before the decision of which he cannot settle his final account. He's ordered by the Court that he be allowed time until the 2nd Tuesday in August next to settle his accounts.

Adjourned till Monday next.

An adjourned Orphans' Court — present the Judge and Register.

George Atkinson of Somerset County in Maryland appears and proves the will of Robert Waters deceased — being a witness thereto.

Letters of Administration on the personal estate of Joseph Hodgson late of Washington County deceased are granted to Rebecca Hodgson of said county his widow, she having given bond &c.

Adjourned to Saturday next.

Saturday 22nd June 1805

The Court meet and adjourns until 27th July next.

Thursday 27th July 1805

An adjourned Orphans' Court &c.

Joseph Commarque of Alexandria County in the District of Columbia having applied for Letters of administration *de bonis non* on the estate of Joseph Bardon late of Montgomery County in Maryland deceased and having filed Bond with approved security for the performance of his duty — Ordered that the said Letters be issued to him unless cause to the contrary be shewn to this court on or before the 2nd Tuesday in October next — provided a copy of this order be published in one of the Baltimore and one of the Philadelphia newspapers once a week for six weeks previous thereto —

William Brown Hodgson and Joseph Hodgson infant children of Joseph Hodgson deceased are brought into Court by their mother Rebecca Hodgson whom the Court appoints as their Guardian — Ordered that she give Bond as to each in the penalty of two thousand dollars. Phineas Bradley and John Eliason are approved as her securities.

Ordered that Rebecca Hodgson administratrix of Joseph Hodgson give notice to Creditors to exhibit their claims, by advertisement in the National Intelligencer three times.

Letters of administration are Granted to Thomas H. Gilliss on the estate of Patrick Lynch — he having given Bond &c.

Ordered that he advertise for creditors to exhibit their claims, three times in the *National Intelligencer*.

Kinsey Gittings, one of the securities of Jane Burch administratrix of Jesse Burch appears and returns, on oath, an Inventory of the personal estate of said Jesse Burch in his hands and prays an order to sell the same. Ordered that he sell the same at public auction, on a credit of six months, on giving three weeks' notice in the *Washington Federalist* taking Bond with approved security for payment with interest.

Charles Glover, acting administrator of John Crookshank appears and passes his first account.

Adjourned to 2nd Tuesday in Augt.

Tuesday (2nd) 13 August 1805

At an Orphans' Court for Washington County —

Present: Wm. H. Dorsey, Esq., Judge — Jno. Hewitt, Regr.

Isaac Owens the executor of Samuel Williams appears and passes his final account of his administration — which is entered on record — in account book.

Samuel N. Smallwood administrator of Richard Frazer deceased appears in Court and states that he has in hands assets to pay the creditors of the deceased who had exhibited their claims agreeably to notice heretofore published, one third of their claims, after deducting all costs and charges of his administration & a debt due the United States (they having a preference) and prays that the same may be distributed under the direction of the Court according to the following list of said claims:

To the United States Navy Department } the full amount of their claim }	177.83
Office of Discount & Deposit, Washington	1053.05

Henry Herford & Son	300.74
Bennet & Watts	292.10
Thomas Young	262.03¾
Cuthbert Powell	211.36
Nicholas Harper	120.28
Charles Glover	105.04
Charles G. Herford	89.04
John P. Lovell	51.13
Rapine, Conrad & Co.	24.80
George St. Clair	19.00
James D. Barry	16.39
William Prout	18.18¾
Samuel Fowler	20.10½

John L. Naylor	23.43¼
Henry Ingle	12.88
Wm. H.P. Tuckfield	9.00
George W. Riggs	40.00
Joel Brown	70.00
Robert Alexander	9.22½
Gustavous Higdon	7.05
[Bailey] Washington	12.70
Francis Deakins	17.68
Wm. Lovell	5.00
Henry Keefer	5.00
Edwd. Eno	2.54
Joseph Johnston	2.45
	$4556.76

All of whom are to receive one third of their respective claims as above stated. Adjourned till 23rd instant.

August 23, 1805

The following order was sent by the Judge to the Register:

Ordered that the administrators of David Rawn sell the personal property of the decd. at public auction giving ten days previous notice of such sale in a newspaper of Washington and of Georgetown on the following terms: For all purchases above twenty dollars on a credit of six months taking Bond with security on interest from the day of sale — All purchases under that sum to be for Cash.

Friday 23rd August 1805

At an adjourned Orphans' Court &c.

William Nelson a poor boy, aged fourteen years on the first day of March last, is brought into Court and is now by the Court placed and bound out as an apprentice to John Long of Georgetown in Washington County, Baker, until he arrives to the age of 21 years — and the said John Long being present in Court agrees to take the said William Nelson as his apprentice, to teach him his said trade of business of a Baker and to find him sufficient meat, drink, washing, cloathing, lodging and other necessaries during said term, and to teach him — common reading, writing and arithmetic.

Adjourn till Saturday 31st inst.

Saturday 31st August 1805

At an adjourned Court were present:

William H. Dorsey, Esq., Judge
John Hewitt, Regr.

No business appearing — the Court adjourned until the Court in course.

A special Orphans' Court at Semmes', Geo'Town, 16 September 1805

Walter Bateman aged seventeen years on the 8th day of June last, an orphan boy, is bound to Henry Keefer of Georgetown — boot & shoe-maker — to serve until 21 years old on usual terms &c. and to be taught reading, writing & arithmetic.

At an adjourned Orphans' Court, 17 Sept. 1805

Present: Wm. H. Dorsey, Esq., Judge: Jno. Hewitt, Regr.

William Howard an orphan boy aged 18 years on the 27th of November next is brought into court by Citation at the instance of Henry Keefer, and it appearing that the said William Howard is destitute of the means of support and that he has been living in the character of an apprentice with said Keefer for 18 months past and upwards, under a verbal agreement and that he had since left the service of aid Keefer without his consent, — and no relation of said William Howard appearing persuant to law to enter into Bond for his maintenance — Bound to Keefer &c.&c. — Keefer to give him 20 dollars at end of his apprent.

Benjamin Howard an orphan boy aged 17 yrs. 16 Feby. last — bound to Henry Keefer, as above &c.

Saturday 28 September 1805

A special Orphans' Court

Letters of administration to Samuel Brown and Mary Jenkins on the estate of William Jenkins.

Charles Windham an orphan boy aged 16 years the seventeenth day of May last brought into Court by James Dawes of Geo: Town and bound to him to learn Boot and shoemaking untill 21 years old — to find common necessaries and teach him common reading, writing and arithmetic — and to find him 16 Dolls. at end of apprenticesp.

John Wayman aged 16 the 25 Jany. last to bound to Dawes on the same terms &c.

Tuesday 8th October 1805

An Orphans' Court holden this day (at Rhodes')

Present: William H. Dorsey, Esq.

Esme Richardson, a poor orphan boy aged fifteen about the first of June last, as near as can be ascertained, bound to James Patterson of the City of Washington, boot and shoemaker — usual necessaries — common reading, writing, and arithmetic — (same as

W. Proctor's 12 Feb. 1805).

Letters adm. d.b.n. to Joseph Commarque on estate of Jean Bardon — late of Montgomery County, Maryland.

Order'd that Saml. Brown and Mary Jenkins admin. William Jenkins, tell & give notice to creditors by advertisement 3 times in Smith's paper. —

Letters to Daniel Carmick on the following person's estate all of the United States Marine Corps, namely:

Alexander Hodges	—	John Needham
John Mathen	—	Aza Pancost
Laurence Marten	—	Henry Norge
Elisha Farnahm	—	Michael McLane
Joseph Chesker	—	Charles Gruber
James Belts	—	William Dailey
Mordicai McCloud	—	John Hubbard
John Willoughby	—	John Frame
Silas Hand	—	John Ekers
Robert Hitchman	—	Nathan Buck
Henry Bannery	—	John Gardner
Barney Grimes	—	Henry Whitesides
James Barrett	—	Francis Henderson
Thomas Wilson	—	Jesse Pearce
	& Peter Pector	

Also to Joseph Tarbell on the estate of David Darling, a marine of said Corps.

Adjd. to Saturday week.

Saturday 2 Novr. 1805

Ordered that Washington Bowie and Henry Wayman administrators of Charles Wayman deceased, sell the personal property of said deceased at public auction giving two weeks previous notice of said sale in the *Washington Federalist*, and that the terms be — for all sums under twenty dollars — cash — all sums above twenty dollars to be for a credit of six months — taking bond with approved security payable with interest from the date.

Ordered that Letters of administration on the personal estate of Christian Slimmer issue to John Bridges he having given bond &c.

Adjd. till Saturday next.

An adjourned Orphans' Court on Saturday 9 Nov. 1805 — (at Rhodes)

Present: William H. Dorsey, Esq., Judge
Jno. Hewitt, Regr.

Maria Thomas the natural child of Minty Thomas, a free mulatto woman, and supposed to be eight years old on the first day of January next is brought into Court by David Shoemaker of Washington County, and is bound by the Court , Apprentice to said

David Shoemaker to serve him as such until she attain the age of sixteen years: the said David Shoemaker present in Court agrees to take the said Maria Thomas as his Apprentice and contracts to teach or have her taught the business of a Housewife and during said term to find and provide her Good and sufficient meat, washing, cloathes, lodging and other necessaries — and to teach her Common reading.

William Brent and Washington Boyd both of Washington County, having applied for Letters of administration on the personal estate of Catharine Johnson of same county deceased — and given satisfactory security — the same are Issued to them.

Tuesday Nov. 12, 1805

A special Orphans' Court &c. — (Rhodes)

Ordered that the administrators of Charles Wayman give notice to Creditors to exhibit their claims on or before the 20th day of May next, by advertisement inserted once a week for four weeks in the *Washington Federalist.*

Adjd.

An adjourned Orphans' Court

Saturday 16 Nov. 1805 — (at Rhodes)

Tobias [Johnson], a free black boy, aged six years on the 24th day of August next is produced in Court by his mother Rachael Johnson, a free black woman — and is, by her consent, placed and bound out as an apprentice to John Dempsie of Washington City and County until the age of twenty one — to serve him as a waiter and the said Jno. Dempsie being present consents to take him as his apprentice and engages to find and sufficiently provide him with good meat &c. — and to have him taught common reading. —

Ordered that the administrators of William Jenkins deceased sell the personal property of the deceased returned in their inventory — on a credit of six months, for all purchases above twenty dollars, taking bonds with security on interest — all purchases under that sum for Cash. They shall give notice of such sale by advertisement three times in the *National Intelligencer.*

On application of Catherine Harrison one of the administrators of William Harrison, ordered that she give notice by advertisement inserted three times in the *Washington Federalist* for Creditors to bring in their claims at the place of session of their court on the 2nd Tuesday of December next, for a distribution of assets under direction of the Court. —

Similar order to John O'Brien administrator of James &c.

William Mackey having applied for Letters of administration on the personal estate of Mary Tennis late of Washington County deceased and given approved security the same are Issued to him.

Henry Ingle having applied for Letters of administration on the personal estate of William H. Smilie late of Washington County deceased and given good security — the same are Granted him.

Letters of administration on the personal estate of Christian Slimmer are granted to John Bridges — he having given Bond.

John Hoye and Leonard M. Deakins, by John Hoye, Executors of Francis Deakins, dec'd. — pass their first account with this Court.

Saturday 23rd Nov. 1805

At a special court &c. — (at W.H. Dorseys) —

Letters of administration on the estate of Nathan Orme late of Montgomery County in Maryland deceased — are Granted in this court to Polly Orme and Basil M. Beall.

Monday 2nd December 1805

At a special Orphans' Court holden this day (at the registers office) —

Alexander Dunlap of the City of New York, having heretofore made application for Letters of administration on the personal estate of John Dunlap late of Washington County dec'd. — his brother — and having filed bond as required by law, with William Patterson and Hugh Thompson of Baltimore as his securities — Letters are this day Granted him. —

Letters to Robert Howison on estate of William Howison of New Orleans. —

Friday 6th December 1805

A special meeting of the Orphans' Court (at Rhodes)

John B. Rittenhouse having heretofore applied for Letters of administration on the personal estate of his decd. brother Benjamin F. Rittenhouse — late of the United States frigate *Constellation* — and having this day given bond with security as required by law — Letters of administration are this day Issued to him.

Ordered that Henry Ingle, administrator of William H. Smilie deceased, sell the personal property of the deceased contained in his inventory. That the sale be at public auction and on a credit of six months on interest for all purchases above twenty dollars taking bond or note with security for payment. Purchases not exceeding 20 dollars to be for Cash. Ten days notice of the sale shall be given by advertisement inserted Three times in the *National Intelligencer*.

Adjd.

Tuesday 10th December 1805

At an Orphans' Court holden for the County of Washington in the City of Washington were present:

William H. Dorsey, Esquire, Judge
John Hewitt, Register. —

Richard Silence a poor boy destitute of the means of support and aged 18 years on the seventh instant is brought into Court and is by the Court placed and bound out as an Apprentice to George Craig of Washington County — bricklayer and Stone-Mason to serve him as such apprentice until the full age of twenty one years And the said George Craig present in Court agrees and contracts to teach his said apprentice his said art or trade of a bricklayer and Stone-mason and to find and provide for him, during his apprenticeship sufficient meat, drink, washing, cloathing, lodging and other necessaries.

The will of Edward Gorman, a seaman late of the United States frigate *Philadelphia* deceased — having been proven before the Court in due form — Letters of Administration *cum Testamento annexo* are Granted to Richard Lyons the sole Legatee — he having entered into bond with approved security as required by Law.

Ordered that Thomas H. Gilliss, executor of Stanley Byus deceased sell the personal property of the deceased at public auction on a credit of six months for all purchases above twenty dollars taking bond and note with good security for payment with interest and that he give notice of such sale in Smith's *National Intelligencer* — Also that he give notice to the Creditors of said Byus to exhibit their claims by advertisement in the usual form, inserted in said paper once a week for two months. —

On application of Sarah Fownes Executrix of John Fownes decd. ordered that she give notice to the Creditors of said decd. — by advertisement inserted three weeks in Smith's *National Intelligencer* and in Gundt and Brown's Baltimore paper to exhibit their claims on the fourth Monday in January next at Rhodes' tavern in the City of Washington between the house of W.A.M. and I.P.M. then and there to receive their dividends of the personal estate of the deceased — under the direction of this Court.

Joseph Simms, a poor boy destitute of the means of support and aged fourteen years the seventeenth day of November last is brought into Court by his mother and with her consent is placed and bound out as an apprentice to John Lutz of Washington County, [Saddler] and Harness maker — to serve him as an apprentice until the age of twenty one years — And the said John Lutz being present in Court agrees and contracts to teach the said Joseph Simms the said art or trade of a Sadler and Harness-maker, to find and provide him sufficient meat, drink, washing, cloathing, lodging and other necessaries — to have him taught common reading, writing and arithmetic and, at the end of his service to give him the sum of twenty six dollars and sixty six cents.

Samuel Brooke, administrator of James Paxton decd. appears and passes his first account. —

Henry Ingle and Shadrach Davis, administrators of Jasper DeCarnap deceased appear and pass their third account.

David Peter, administrator of Thomas Wilson decd. appears and passes his first account.

Application is made, by Thomas Herty of Washington County for Letters of administration on the estate of John Prentice late of United States frigate *Constellation* deceased.

Adjourned til tomorrow —

At an adjourned Orphans' Court on Wednesday the 11th December 1805 — present as yesterday —

Catherine Harrison, administratrix of James Harrison appears and passes her first account.

15th January 1806

At a special Orphans' Court (at Rhodes)

Present: Wm. H. Dorsey, Esq., Judge — Jno. Hewitt, Regr.

Walter T. [Greenfield] having heretofore applied for Letters of administration on the personal estate of George Beall late of Washington County deceased and having produced the widow's renunciation in writing and entered into Bond with security as required by law — Letters of administration on said estate are Granted him.

Ordered that Walter T. Greenfield administration of George Beall deceased Give notice to Creditors to exhibit their claims by advertisement in the usual form inserted once a week for three successive weeks in Smith's *National Intelligencer*.

Adjourn'd.

21 January 1806

At a special Orphan's Court at Graham's Tavern in Georgetown —
Present the Judge and Register —

Letters of Administration are Granted to William Leith on the personal estate of John Prentice he having entered into Bond &c.

Adjourn'd.

Monday 27th January 1806

Pursuant to notice Sarah Fownes Executrix of John Fownes appears to make a dividend of assets in hand Sundry claims were exhibited — When the same was postponed —

Monday 3rd February 1806

At a special Orphan's Court, at the house of Abner Ritchie in George-Town were present:

William H. Dorsey, Esq., Judge
John Hewitt, Register

Abner Ritchie and Charles A. Beatty, administrators of Charles Beatty deceased appear and pass their First account.

Daniel Busserd, administrator of Martin Whelan decd. appears and passes his first account.

Adjourned.

Tuesday 11th February 1806 (2 Tuesday) —

The Judge having not attended the Register adjourns the Court until Monday next -

Monday 17th February 1806

The Court meets — Present Will. H. Dorsey, Esq., Judge — and John Hewitt — Register No business reads the Court adjourns until Saturday 1st March next

Saturday 1st March 1806

At an Adjourned Orphans' Court holden &c. were present the Judge and Register

Application is made by William Thompson for Letters of administration on the personal estate of William Jackson deceased.

Application is made by Matthew Brown for Letters of administration on the personal estate of James Williams deceased.

William Austin Reeder an orphan boy destitute of the means of support and aged eleven years on the eleventh instant is brought into Court and is placed and bound and by the Court as an apprentice to William King of Georgetown in Washington County, Cabinet maker to serve him until the age of twenty one years, and the said William King present in Court agrees and contracts to teach the said William A. Reeder his said trade in art of a Cabinet-maker — to find and provide him sufficient meat, drink, cloathing, washing, lodging and other necessaries and to teach him common reading, writing & arithmetic.

Robert Sandford an orphan boy destitute of the means of support and aged sixteen years the 15th of November last is brought into Court and is placed and bound out, by the Court as an apprentice to Isaac Owens of Washington County — House carpenter and Joiner, to serve him to said trade until the age of twenty one years: — And the said Isaac Owens being present in Court agrees and contracts on his part, to teach the said Robert Sandford his said art or trade of a House-Carpenter and joiner, to find and provide him sufficient meat, drink, washing, cloathing, lodging and other necessaries, to have him instructed in common reading, writing and arithmetic and, at the end of his apprenticeship to give him a lot of Bench-Tools and the sum of Five pounds Maryland currency. —

Samuel Butler, a black-boy, the natural child of Rebecca Butler, aged 12 years as nearly as can be ascertained — (bound to said Isaac Owens &c. — on the same terms as above.)

Letters of Administration on the personal estate of John Boyce late of Washington County deceased are Granted to Sarah Boyce his widow — she having entered into Bond pursuant to law and taken the oath of office. Ordered that she give notice to Creditors to exhibit their claims against the deceased by advertisement in the usual form inserted once a week for three successive weeks in the *National Intelligencer*.

Letters of administration are Granted to John Johnson — on the personal estates of the following persons, viz:

of Levi White of the United States Marine Corps
of Edward Stewart — of the same Corps
of John Wilton — of the same Corps

He having, in each case entered into bond with approved securities as required by law and taken the oath of office.

Letters of administration issued (by the Register) to Samuel Duvall on the personal estate of Mary Duvall late of Washington County deceased — he having entered into bond with good security as required by law and taken the oath of office.

Adjourned until Tuesday next —

Tuesday 4th March 1806

At an adjourned Orphans' Court holden &c.

Present: Wm. H. Dorsey, Esq., Judge — Jno. Hewitt, Regr.

James Clarke a poor boy aged thirteen years on the 8th day of August next, is brought into Court by his mother Mary Clarke, and with his mother's consent, is placed and bound out, by the Court, as an apprentice to Benjamin Davies of George-town, Washington County — Taylor — to serve him, as such until he attain the age of twenty one years: — And the said Benjamin Davies being present in Court agrees and contracts to teach the said James Clarke his said Trade of a Taylor, and to provide him sufficient meats, drink, cloathing, lodging and other necessaries and to have him taught common reading, writing and arithmetic —

Adjourned til Saturday next.

Saturday 8th March 1806

The Judge attends and adjourns the Court until the Court in course —

Tuesday (2nd in the month) 8 April 1806

Letters of administration issued to Peggy McLaughlin on the estate of Charles McLaughlin deceased in pursuance of Orders of 5th April from William H. Dorsey, Esq., and tested on 5th April.

In the absence of the Judge, the Register meets and adjourns the Court until the Court in course —

Registered.

* * * * * * * * * * * * *

[Included at the back of the book is a loose paper with the following]

Mr. Roach:

Sir please give the bearer the copy of Mr. J.P. Garmon's will, and he will pay you two Dollars and thirteen cents for the same and oblige yours. M. Quigly

June 23rd 1849.

[end of record]

Minutes of the Proceedings of the Orphans' Court of Washington County Commencing the 29th of April 1806 ending 10 September 1808 Washington City

At an Orphans' County [sic] for Washington County in the District of Columbia, holden on Tuesday the 29th day of April 1806 at Rhodes' Hotel in the City of Washington were present:

Robert Brent, Esquire, Judge
John Hewitt, Register of Wills

Robert Brent, Esquire, produces his Commission as Judge from the President of the United States in the following words viz:

Thomas Jefferson President of the United States of America, To all who shall see these presents Greeting:

Know ye That reposing special Trust and confidence in the wisdom, uprightness and learning of Robert Brent of the Territory of Columbia, I have nominated and by and with the advice and consent of the Senate, Do appoint him Judge of the Orphans' Court for the County of Washington in the District of Columbia, and do authorize and empower him to execute and fulfil the duties of that office according to the Constitution and laws of the United States; and to Have and To Hold the said Office, with all the powers, privileges and emoluments to the same of right appertaining unto him the said Robert Brent during his good behaviour.

[seal] In Testimony whereof, I have caused these Letters to be made patent and the seal of the United States to be hereunto affixed.

Given under my hand at the City of Washington the sixteenth day of April in the year of our Lord one thousand, eight hundred and six; and of the Independence of the United States of America the thirtieth —

Tho: Jefferson

By the President
James Madison
Secretary of State

[page 2]

The said Robert Brent, Esq., also produces a certificate of his qualification by taking his oath of office in the following words viz:

I Robert Brent do solemnly promise and swear that as Judge of the Orphans' Court of Washington County in the District of Columbia, I will do equal right and Justice according to the law of the United States in every case in which I shall act as Judge of the Orphans' Court aforesaid — freely without sale and fully without denial and speedily without delay and will behave myself justly, honestly, and faithfully in the said office, according to the best of my knowledge and understanding, so help me God.

Robert Brent

District of Columbia, Washington County Ct. —

The foregoing oath was this day administered by me to Robert Brent, Esq., as Judge of the Orphans' Court of Washington County in the District of Columbia — April 28t 1806 —

William Thornton, Just. peace

Eliza Rawn acting administratrix of David Rawn deceased appears and passes their first and final account of their administration of the personal estate of the said deceased and it appearing to the Court that after the payment of all acts, charges and debts, there remains, in the hands of the administrators, the sum of four hundred and twenty seven dollars and eighty one cents — It is Ordered by the Court that the said balance be distributed as follows: — one third thereof to the said Eliza Rawn as widow of the deceased, and the remaining two thirds be distributed among Juliana Rawn, Charles Cotesworth Rawn and David Rawn, the children of the deceased —

Ordered also that said Eliza Rawn be and she hereby is appointed Guardian of the persons and property of her infant children under the age of fourteen years, namely Juliana Rawn, [page] Charles Cotesworth Rawn and David Rawn and that she entered into bonds with good securities, as required by law, for the performance of her duty as Guardian, as to each of said children —

Matthew Brown of Washington County in the District of Columbia having heretofore applied for Letters of administration on the personal estate of James Williams late of the United States ship *United States*, seaman deceased and having given bond with approved securities as required by law, the said Letters are now Granted him as a creditor —

William Thompson of Washington County in the District of Columbia having heretofore applied for Letters of administration on the personal estate of William Jackson late of the United States ship the *John Adams* — captain's clerk, deceased — and having Given bond with approved securities as required by law — the said Letters are now granted him as a Creditor —

The court adjourned until Saturday next.

Saturday 3rd of May 1806

At an Orphan's Court holden for Washington County in the District of Columbia on Saturday the 3rd day of May 1806 at Rhodes's Hotel in the City of Washington, present:

Robert Brent, Esq., Judge

John Hewitt, Regr.

Thomas Herty of Washington County having heretofore applied for Letters of administration on the personal estate of James Kirby an ordinary seaman late of the United States ship *The Constellation* deceased — and having this day entered into Bond with approved securities for the faithful performance of his duty, according to law — the said Letters are Granted to him —

The court adjourns until Saturday next.

[page 4]

Monday 4 May 1806

Daniel Rapine having applied for Letters of administration on the personal estate of Susanna Osborn of Washington County deceased (in right of his wife) and having produced the renunciations in writing of Martha Osborn and Mary Osborn in his favor and given Bond with security as prescribed by law — Letters were this day issued to him — the oath of office administered and a warrant of appraisement issued —

Thursday 8th May 1806

John C. Love of Washington County having applied for Letters of administration on the estate of William Allen late of the United States Marine Corps deceased, as a Creditor, and having given bond with approved security as required by law — letters of administration are this day issued to him, by order of the Judge — as follows — Grant letters of administration to Mr. John C. Love on the estate of William Allen late of the United States Marine Corps — the securities offered are deemed sufficient to wit Robt. Rankin & John Johnson —

Robt. Brent

Mr. Hewitt May 5th 1806

Saturday 10th May 1806

At an adjourned Orphans' Court holden on Saturday the 10th day of May 1806, were present: Robert Brent, Esq., Judge
John Hewitt, Regr. Wills

Ordered that Daniel Rapine, administrator of Susanna Osborn deceased give notice to the Creditors of the deceased to exhibit their claims by advertisement inserted once a week for three successive weeks in a Washington City and a Baltimore newspaper —

[page]

William Brent of Washington County, having applied for Letters of administration on the personal estate of Peter Healey of said County deceased and having Given Bond with approved security — Letters of administration are issued to him — as Creditor —

John McLeod ~~having~~ of Prince George's County in Maryland — having applied for Letters of administration on the personal estate of his brother William McLeod late of the United States frigate *Constellation* deceased — and having given Bond with approved security the said Letters are now Granted him.

Rebecca Hodgson administratrix of Joseph Hodgson appears and returns a List of Debts, one to &c. money belong to the deceased.

Court adjourned till this day week.

14 May 1806

George French the Executor produced the will of Margret Scott of Washington County deceased & the same was proven by said French and Isabella Scott a witness — and said George having entered into Bond with securities &c. Letters Testamentary are this day issued to him —

Saturday 17th May 1806

At an Orphans' Court holden this day &c. present:

Robert Brent, Esq., Judge
Jno. Hewitt, Regr.

Margaret Fenwick the infant child of Bennett Fenwick decd. aged seven years the 5th of February next is brought into Court by her mother Mary Ann Fenwick and the said Mary Ann Fenwick is appointed Guardian of the person & property of said infant.

Thomas G. Slye of Washington County District of Columbia and Raphael Boarman of Charles County in Maryland are approved as securities in the Bond — [page 6]

Ann Bradley, administratrix of William Bradley appeared and passes her first account.

Alexander Cochran Junior having applied for Letters of administration on the personal estate of John Pitman Lovell late of Washington County deceased — and having produced an attested renunciation of Rachel Lovell the widow of the deceased & given Bond with securities as required by law — Letters are Granted him —

Ordered that Alexander Cochran Jr. administrator of John P. Lovell deceased, give notice to the Creditors of the deceased to exhibit their claims, by advertisement in the *National Intelligencer* — inserted once a week for three successive weeks —

Court adjourns till Saturday next.

Saturday 24th May 1806

The Register attends but the Judge not appearing the Court is adjourned untill Saturday next.

Letters of administration are issued to John Johnson of Washington County as a Creditor — on the personal estate of Doctor Starling Archer late of the Navy of the United States — he having entered into Bond with security &c. — [page]

Saturday 31st May 1806

At an Orphan's Court holden this day (at Rhodes's) were present—

Robert Brent, Esq., Judge
John Hewitt, Register of Wills

~~Ordered~~ James R. Dermott late of Washington County deceased having by his last will and testament appointed James Barry, William Hartshorn & James Dardis Guardians of his infant children John, Ann and James Dermott — and the said Guardians having refused to take upon themselves the execution of the trust — Alice Dermott the widow of said James R. Dermott is appointed Guardian of the persons and property of said John, Ann and James Dermott —

Benjamin James and Mary James of Stafford County, Virginia are approved of as securities — Ordered that they enter into bond with the said Alice Dermott in the penalty of two thousand dollars — for the performance of their duty of Guardian[s], as required by law.

Ordered that the said Alice Dermott apply the whole rents and annual proceeds of the property of said infants (after deducting her own share) towards the maintenance and education of the said infants —

The court adjourns till 2nd Tuesday in June.

Tuesday 10 June 1806

At an Orphans' Court holden this day being the regular stated meeting —

The Register attends — but the Judge not attending, the register pursuant to power vested in him by law, adjourns the court until Saturday the 21st instant. [page]

Saturday 21st June 1806

At an adjourned Orphans' Court were present: Robert Brent, Esq., Judge
John Hewitt, Regr.

Vachael Brown a poor boy, aged about 12 years as nearly as can be ascertained is brought into Court by the reverent Robert Elliot of the City of Washington — and it appearing to the court that the said Vachael is without the mean[s] of support and that he is willing and desirous to be bound out as an apprentice to the said Robert Elliot the said Vachael Brown is bound and placed as an apprentice to the said Robert Elliot until he attain the age of twenty one years — the said Robert Elliot consents to take the said boy as his apprentice — to learn the business of a House servant — and hereby agrees to teach or cause him to be instructed in the said business — to find and provide him the necessaries of life and to teach him common reading, writing and arithmetic — & further that he will comply, conform to & with all engagements heretofore entered into by him — when said boy was bound in Maryland —

The court adjourns until Saturday next. [page]

26 June 1806

Letters of Administration are issued by the register to Dorothy Repley on the estate of John Repley Madison of the United States' Navy.

Saturday 28th June 1806

At an adjourned Orphans' Court was present Robert Brent, Esq., Judge — who adjourns the court to next Saturday —

Persuant to the order of the Judge, Letters are issued this day by the register to Teresa Scott on the estate of her husband James Scott of Washington County deceased.

Saturday 5th July 1806

At an adjourned Orphans' Court holden this day were present:

Robert Brent, Esquire, Judge
Jno. Hewitt, Regr. of Wills

Application having heretofore been made by Mary Spalding for Letters o administration on the personal estate of her husband William Spalding late of Washingtor County deceased, and having entered into bond with approved securities as required b law the same are this day granted her by the Court.

~~Christiana Berry, by Thomas Herty her attorney, makes application for Letters o administration on the personal estate of William [Sykes] late of Washington Count deceased, as an Executor~~ — [page 10]

Nace a yellow boy aged about 10 years on the 8th day of April last is brought int Court and is bound, by the Court, to William Fields of Georgetown, Washington County Bricklayer and Plaisterer to serve him until the age of 21 years — and the said Willian Fields agrees to teach the said Nace his said trade of a Bricklayer and plaisterer, to fin and provide him sufficient meat &c. — to each or have him taught common reading, writin and arithmetic — and at the end of his apprenticeship to give him a suit of cloaths of th value of 24 dollars — and complete set of tools —

Lewis Fletcher an orphan coloured boy aged 14 years the first day of March last i brought into Court by Henry Fleet of Washington County — Boot and Shoemaker — an is, with his own consent, bound out, by the Court, as an apprentice to said Henry Fleet t serve him as such until he attain the full age of twenty one years — And the said Henr Fleet, being present in court, consents to take the said ~~William~~ Lewis Fletcher as hi apprentice — and [?] to teach or cause to be taught the said art or trade of a Boot an Shoemaker — to find and provide him sufficient meat &c. to be taught common reading writing and arithmetic and at the end of his apprenticeship to give him a new suit of clothe with 24 dollars and a complete set of Tools —

Howe Adams an orphan black boy destitute of the means of support, aged 18 year — the [blank] day of [blank] is brought into Court by Henry Fleet of Washington County &c — him (as in former except that he is to give $50). [page]

On the application by Christiana Berry for Letters of administration on the persona estate of William Sykes late of the Navy of the United States, seaman, deceased — claiming the same as a creditor — Ordered that she give notice of her said application b advertisement in the *National Intelligencer* inserted once a week for four weeks —

Adjourned until Saturday next.

Saturday 12th July 1806

At an adjourned Orphans' Court were present: Robert Brent, Esq., Judge
John Hewitt, Regr. of Wills

On the application of Michael McCormick for Letters of administration on th personal estate of William Gough late of the Navy of the United States, seaman, decease — claiming the same as a Creditor — Ordered that he give notice of his said applicatio by advertisement in the *National Intelligencer* inserted once a week for four weeks —

Sarah Fownes executrix of John Fownes appears and passes her second account nd it appearing that there is a balance of @1243.60½ due by her as executrix Order'd that he distribute the same among the Creditors in proportion to their claims are here fore xhibited — the same amounting to 13 8/10 cents in the Dollar — [page 12]

Robert Maitland an orphan boy aged nine years on the 9th day of October next is rought into court by James Maitland of Washington County and is placed out and bound y the Court, as an apprentice to said James Maitland to learn the trade of a Bricklayer and tone-Mason — and the said James Maitland being present in court, agrees to take the aid Robert Maitland as his apprentice and engages to teach him the said trade of a ricklayer and Stone Mason — to find and provide him, during his apprenticeship, sufficient ıeat, drink, washing, cloathing and other necessaries — and to teach him common eading, writing and arithmetic. At the end of his apprenticeship to give him a new suit of loathes worth, at least, 24 dollars.

The court adjourns till Saturday next.

.t an Orphans' Court on Saturday the 19 July 1806 were present:

Robt. Brent, Esq., Judge
Jno. Hewitt, Regr.

Letters of administration issued to Henrietta Vermillion on estate of John Vermillion ıte of said County — deceased.

Court adjourns until Saturday next. [page]

July 26th 1806

t an adjourned Orphans' Court were present:

Robert Brent, Esq., Judge
John Hewitt, Regr. Wills

Dr. William Thornton having as executor proved the will of Mary E. Robinson late f Washington County decd. & filed Bond with approved securities — Letters Testamentary re this day issued to him —

The following petition was this day exhibited by Peggy McLaughlin

To his honor Robert Brent Esquire Judge of the Orphans Court for the County of Vashington in the District of Columbia — The petition of Peggy McLaughlin Administratrix f Charles McLaughlin deceased represents:

That your petitioner has not been able to return a list of debts sperate and desperate c.&c. (see the filed petition) —

Ordered that Ann Hurdle, administratrix of Leonard Hurdle give notice to Creditors exhibit their claims by advertisement in the usual form, inserted four times in the *National ıtelligencer*. [page]

July 29th 1806

George Hodge[s] (of the Navy Yard) applies for administration on the estate of ryan Tweedy — late Boatswains yeoman, on board the frigate *Essex* — who died at

Malaga. The deceased has a wife named Betsy in Philadelphia — & his application is made to prevent others not entitled —

Saturday 2nd August 1806

At an adjourned Orphans' Court — the Register attends — and the judge being absent — adjourns the court until Saturday next.

Monday 4th August 1806

Application made by Mary Cahill for Letters of administration on the estate of Daniel Cahill late a marine belonging to the *Essex* frigate —

Saturday 9 Augt. 1806

At an adjourned Orphans' Court this day were present: Robert Brent, Esq., Judge
John Hewitt, Register

The executors of David Rutherford are order'd and directed to advertise for the Creditors of the deceased to being in their claims by the 13th of March next — said notice to be inserted in the *National Intelligencer* four times — [page]

David Yeates an orphan boy aged, as nearly as can be ascertained, 10 years on the 11th day of June past, is brought into court and with his own and his mother's consent, is bound to the reverend Leonard Neale of Washington County — to serve him as an apprentice until 21 years — and the said Leonard Neale present in Court agrees to take him said David Yeates as his apprentice — to teach or have him taught some good mechanical trade — to find and provide him sufficient meat, drink, clothing and other necessaries — to teach him common reading, writing and arithmetic — and a good suit of cloathes worth at least 22 dollars.

Letters to Mary Cahil on estate of Daniel Cahil.

To William Prince on the estate of James Lovell

Court adjourns till Tuesday next —

Tuesday (2nd) — August 12th 1806 —

The Court meets — present the Judge and register & adjourns untill Saturday next

2nd acct. Ch. A. Beatty's adminors.

Saturday 16th August 1806

The Judge attends and in the absence of the register, adjourns until Saturday next. [page]

Augt. 20, 1806

Application is made by George Brown for Letters of administration on the personal estate of his brother John T. Brown.

August 23rd 1806. Letters are Granted to him this day — accordingly —

Saturday 23rd August 1806

At an adjourned Orphans' Court this day the Register attends, and in the absence of the Judge who does not attend, adjourns the Court until Saturday next —

Monday 25th August 1806

George Hodges having applied for Letters of administration on the personal estate of Bryan Tweedy late Boatswain's yeoman in the frigate *Essex* — and having produced a power of attorney from Elizabeth the wife of said Bryan Tweedy — with a certificate of her marriage — And also a Bond with securities approved of by the Judge, as required by law — Letters are this day issued to him.

Application is made, by David Whann, for Letters of administration on the estate of William Gold — seaman — Nathaniel Holding — seaman — and Luco Benoca, seaman — Arthur Rigway a marine — Thomas Smallwood a marine — Jacob Gilmor — a marine — all of the *Essex* — (Jno. Willing) James Ingerson. [page]

Saturday 30th August 1806

At an adjourned Orphans' Court this day were present: Robert Brent, Esq., Judge
John Hewitt, Regr. of Wills

Horatio Scott, a poor boy destitute of the means of support, aged fourteen years on the 22nd day of February next is brought into Court by his mother Mary Ann Scott & William Thompson — and ~~is~~ with the consent of his said mother is placed and bound out, by the Court, to the said William Thompson of Georgetown in Washington County as an apprentice to the trade of a Copper-Smith and Tin-plate worker, until he attain the ful age of twenty one years — And the said William Thompson agrees, on his part, to teach and instruct the said Horatio Scott or cause him to be taught and instructed his said trade or art of a Coppersmith and Tinplate-worker — to find and provide him, during his apprenticeship, sufficient meat, drink, cloathing, washing and other necessaries — to have him instructed in common reading, writing and arithmetic and to give him, at the end of his apprenticeship a new suit of cloaths worth at least 20 dollars in cash at the option of said apprentice—

James Patterson of Washington County, having produced a power of attorney from William Gough authorizing him to administer on the personal estate of William Gough his nephew late of Washington County, seaman deceased, and having given bond with security as required by law — Letters of administration on the estate of the said William Gough deceased are this day granted to the said James Patterson. [page]

Ordered, on the application of Michael McCormick for Letters of administration on the personal estate of Hugh McCormick late of the Navy of the United States, seaman deceased, that he publish notice of his said application by advertisement in the *National Intelligencer* inserted once a week for four successive weeks.

The Court adjourned until Saturday next.

Saturday 6th September 1806

The Register attends and adjourns the Court in the absence of the Judge, until Saturday next.

Letters of administration are this day issued by the order of the Judge to Christiana Berry on the estate of William Sykes late of the Navy of the United States, seaman deceased.

Letters Testamentary issued by the Register to John Chappell the executor therein named on the will of Margaret Masters late of Washington County deceased.

Application made by David Jamie for Letters of administration on the Estates of the persons applied for by David Whann on 25 Aug. & also on estate of John G. Garraland.

12th Sept. 1806

The will of Joseph Taylor late of Washington County deceased is this day exhibited & proven before the Register — and Letters Testamentary thereon issued to John Davidson and Washington Boyd the executors therein named — [page]

Saturday 13th September 1806

At an adjourned Orphans' Court this day were present:

Robert Brent, Esquire, Judge
John Hewitt, Register of Wills

Nicolas deCowze a poor boy a native of Fessel in Spain & having no parents in the United States, aged ~~fifteen~~ sixteen years about the first of January next as nearly as can be ascertained, is brought into court by Charles Nourse of Washington County and, with his own consent, is placed and bound by the court as an apprentice to the said Charles Nourse to serve him until the age of twenty one years in the Capacity of a waiting man & servant. The said Charles Nourse agrees to take the said Nicholas deCowze [sic] as his apprentice to have him instructed in the necessary and usual duties and qualifications of a waiting man and servant — to find and provide him sufficient meat, drink, cloathing, washing, lodging and other necessaries and, at the end of his service, to give him a suit of cloats [sic] worth at least 22 dollars.

Ordered that John Davidson and Washington Boyd, Executors of Joseph Taylor deceased give notice to the Creditors of said deceased to exhibit their claims — by advertisement inserted in the *National Intelligencer*, once a week for four successive weeks.

Ordered also that the said Executors sell the personal estate of said Taylor contained in the inventory returned by them. That the said sale be on a credit of thee months for all purchases above 20 Dollars taking bonds or notes with good security on interest from the day of sale: all sales amounts to & under 20 dollars to be for cash; [illegible] public notice of said sale to be given by advertisement in said paper [page] inserted at least three times before the day of sale.

Adjourned till [blank]

Thursday September 18th 1806

Mary Hanifiend a poor girl aged twelve years is brought into court by her father Timothy Hanifiend and with his consent is placed and bound out by the Court as an apprentice to John Lowry of Washington County to serve him until the age of sixteen years — And the said John Lowry agrees to take her as his apprentice — & to instruct her in the business of Housewifery to find and provide her good and sufficient accommodations and necessaries & to teach her common reading and writing [copy delivd. paid].

Saturday 20th September 1806

At an adjourned meeting of the Orphans' Court the Register attends, but the Judge not attending, adjourns until Monday next —

Monday 22nd September 1806

At an adjourned Orphans' Court this day were present:

Robert Brent, Esq., Judge
John Hewitt, Regr. Wills

Rebecca Hodgson appears and passes her first account as administratrix of Joseph Hodgson.

On the application of Peggy McLaughlin administratrix of Charles McLaughlin deceased, Ordered that she sell at auction the Personal property of the decussate Contained in the Inventory — That the sale be on a credit of six months for all sums above 20 dollars taking Bonds or notes with Good security on interest from [page] the day of sale, Sales not exceeding 20 dollars to be for Cash. — At least two weeks notice shall be given of the time, place & terms of sale by advertisement in the *National Intelligencer* and *Washington Federalist* and in hand bills set up at public places —

Adjourned untill Saturday next.

Application made by letter 20 Septr. 1806 by Richard B. Gardiner for letters of administration of the estate of John F. Hardey.

Saturday 27th September 1806

At an adjourned Orphan's Court, this day were present:

Robt. Brent, Esq., Judge
John Hewitt, Regr. Wills

John Creighton a poor boy whose parents are unable to support him, aged thirteen years on the first of January next is brought into the Court by Elias Travers of Washington City and County, Baker and is places and bound by the Court as an apprentice to the said Elias Travers until he attain the age of twenty one years — The said Travers being present agrees to take the said John Creighton as his apprentice and to teach him or cause him

[?] his said trade of a Baker, to find and provide him good and sufficient necessaries and support during his apprenticeship — and to teach him common reading, writing and arithmetic — & to give him, at the end of his time a suit of cloathes worth at least 22 dollars, or that sum in money at the option of said boy —

William Hudson an orphan boy aged about fourteen years brought into court by [Elias] Travers &c. — and bound upon the same terms — &c.

Letters of Administration granted to Henry Knowles as a creditor, on the estate of Nathaniel Wilkins, of the State of Maryland. [page]

Richard T. Spalding son of Enoch Spalding aged 18 years on the 5th day of November next, is produced in court by his father — and with his fathers' and his own consent, is placed and bound out by the court as an apprentice to Ebenezer Nesmith of Washington City and County, Carpenter and Joiner to serve him, as such, until he attain the full age of twenty one years. And the said Ebenezer Nesmith, being present in court, agrees to take the said Richard T. Spalding as his apprentice — to teach him or cause him to be taught his said trade or art of a Carpenter & Joiner — to find and provide him good & sufficient necessaries and support during his apprenticeship — to give him at least two months night schooling — and, at the end of his time to give him a set of Bench Tools and a suit of cloathes worth, at least 22 dollars.

Isaiah Lenman aged 19 years on the 18th day of March next is produced in court by his mother and with his own and mothers' consent is placed and bound out by the court as an apprentice to Ebenezer Nesmith of &c. &c. until 21 — (three months night schooling), two at Nesmith's Expence —

(Dunlaps receipts &c.)

Adjourned until Saturday next.

Saturday 4 October 1806

At an adjourned Orphans' Court this day were present:

Robert Brent, Esq., Judge — & Jno. Hewitt, Regr.

Letters of administration on the estate of Hugh McCormick late of the Navy of the United States, seaman deceased are this day issued to Michael McCormick of Washington County, he having entered in bond &c. as required by law —

Adjourns until Saturday next. [page]

Saturday 11th October 1806

At an adjourned Orphans' Court — the Judge and register attend and further adjourn the same until the court in course —

Tuesday (being 2nd in the month) 14 October 1806

The Court meets — present Judge and register and adjourn until Saturday next —

Saturday 18th October 1806

At an adjourned Orphans' Court holden this day were present:

Robert Brent, Esq., Judge
John Hewitt, Regr. of Wills

Martha Wade, widow of Peter Wade, applies for letters of administration on the estate of her said husband.

Letters of administration are Granted to Gerard Gibson on the personal estate of Jane Kissick late of Washington County deceased —

Peggy McLaughlin administratrix of Charles McLaughlin appears and returns a List of Debts.

William Steuart, administrator *cuml.a.* of Mary Dulany appears and passes his final account.

John Peter administrator of John Peter deceased appears and passes his First account.

The court adjourns until Saturday next. [page]

Thursday 23rd October 1806

At a special Orphans' Court holden in and for Washington County at the City of Washington were present: Robert Brent, Esquire, Judge
John Hewitt, Register of Wills —

The following petition was filed on the 22nd instant to wit "To the Honorable Robert Brent, Esq., &c. &c. subscribed John and Geo. Baltzer, Geo. King & Co., Benjn. Patterson, Adam King & Co., John Ott, John Maffet, Ninian Magruder, Ross & Pleasanton, Charles A. Burnett, Wm. Marbury — whereupon the following summons was issued to wit The United States &c.

And now at this day the said Peggy McLaughlin administratrix appears in obedience to the said summons as did also the said petitioners — and the said Peggy McLaughlin presented and filed with the court the petition and demand following to wit — "To the honorable Robert Brent, Esq., &c. — and prays the court to direct a plenary proceeding on said petition — which is granted by the court and time given to the said parties until Friday the 31st instant —

The following Interrogatives were exhibited and filed by the Petitioners, viz. "[blank]

Saturday 25th October 1806

At an adjourned Orphans' Court were present Robert Brent, Esq., Judge — John Hewitt register of wills —

Daniel Rapine administrator of Susanna ~~Holmes~~ Osborn deceased, having this day returned an Inventory of the Goods and chattels of the deceased and having prayed a sale thereof —

Ordered that he sell the said goods and chattels at public auction giving three months credit for all sums above twenty dollars and taking Bonds or notes with good security for payment with interest from the day of sale. Sales not exceeding that sum to

be for cash. At least ten days notice of the sale shall be given in the *National Intelligencer*
[page]

Letters of administration are Granted and issued to David Dobbins on the estate of Daniel Eldridge late of Washington County Gunner in the public service deceased, as a Creditor — he having entered into Bond with securities as required by law —

Washington Bowie one of the administrators of Charles Wayman deceased appears and passes his first account of their administration —

The court adjourns until Friday next.

Friday 31st October 1806

At an adjourned Orphans' Court for Washington County were present: Robert Brent, Esq., Judge — John Hewitt, register of wills.

The court adjourns until tomorrow 10 o'clock.

Saturday 1st November 1806

At an adjourned Orphans' Court for Washington County this day were present:
Robert Brent, Esq., Judge
John Hewitt, register of Wills —

Peggy McLaughlin administratrix of Charles McLaughlin appears by Philip B. Key her attorney on the Citation of John and George Baltzer and others Creditors of said Charles McLaughlin — and craves a continuance of said cause until the 2nd Tuesday in December next which is Granted her.

Robert Underwood acting Executor of John Smith and Robert Underwood Executors of Mark Stockwell deceased appears and passes a second and final account of their administration —

— It appearing by the final account of Robert Underwood and John Smith Executors of Mark Stockwell deceased that there remains a balance of 330 dollars and forty five cents in their hands subject to distribution ordered that the same be paid over and distributed agreeably to the directions of the will of said Mark Stockwell — [page]

Saturday 8th November 1806

The Judge not attending the Register adjourns the court until Saturday next —

Saturday 15th November 1806

The court meets, present Robert Brent, Esq., Judge
Jno. Hewitt, register

Ignatius Downes an Orphan boy aged seventeen years the 7th day of October last is produced in court and with his own consent is placed and bound as an apprentice to Robert Dillon of the City of Washington wheelwright — to serve him until he attain the age of twenty one to the said trade or art of a wheelright [sic] — and the said Robert Dillon agrees to teach the said Ignatius Downes his said trade or art of a wheelwright — to provide and finish him with sufficient meat, drink, ~~washing~~, cloathing, washing and other necessaries — to teach him common reading, writing & arithmetic — and at the end of his time to give him in addition to his ordinary apparel, a new suit of clothes and a set of working Tools of the value of 10 Dollars at least —

William [Mackey], administrator of Mary Tennis deceased, appears and passes his First account —

Hanson Ellis an Orphan Boy aged fourteen years as nearly as can be ascertained is produced in court and with his own consent is placed and bound out as an apprentice to Samuel Hutchenson of Washington City — to serve him until he attain the age of twenty one years and the said Samuel Hutchenson agrees and contracts to teach the said Hanson Ellis or cause him to be taught the business or trade of a Baker — to find and provide him sufficient meat, drink, cloathing, washing, lodging and other necessaries — to teach him common reading, writing and arithmetic — and, at the end of his time to give him, in addition to his ordinary apparel, a new suit of cloaths worth at least twenty dollars.

William Steuart, administrator of Mary Dulany deceased appears and passes his first and final account.

Adjourns till Saturday next. [page]

Nov. 20th

Application by Jekiel [Crossfield] for Letters adm. on estate of Seth Carter — of the Navy.

Saturday 22 Novr. 1806

The register of Wills attends and in the absence of the Judge, adjourns the court until Saturday next.

Saturday 29th Novr. 1806

The court meets — present Robt. Brent, Judge
John Hewitt, regr. Wills

The court adjourns until Monday next.

Monday 1st of December 1806

The court meets present Robt. Brent, Esq., Judge
Jno. Hewitt, Reg. Wills

Betty Huddleston daughter of Joseph Huddleston of Washington County appears in court and makes choice of said Joseph Huddleston as her Guardian of her person and property.

Letters of administration granted and issued to Mary Horolan on the personal estate of her deceased husband Dennis Horolan late of Washington City decd.

Letters Testamentary granted and issued to Robert Getty on last Will of William Irvin late of Washington County deceased.

Letters of administration are Granted and issued to Solomon Stinger on the estate of his brother John Stinger late of Washington City deceased.

Adjourns. [page]

James Williams aged eighteen years on the 15th of September last is bound with the approbation of his mother E. Williams as an apprentice to Thomas Adams until he arrives at the age of twenty one years to learn the Trade of a Turner & Chair maker -- said Adams agrees to give him good and sufficient cloathes, lodging, died and other necessaries during said time, to send him to school so as to have him taught reading, writing and arithmetic and at the end of his time to give him tools to the amount of at least ten dollars and a suit of cloathes of the value of Twenty two dollars or that amount in cash.

John Reeder aged twenty years on the 24th day of November last is bound by the Court as an apprentice to Thomas Adams, to serve him until he arrives at the age of twenty one years and to learn the trade of a Turner -- the said Adams to find him good and sufficient cloathes, lodging, diet, and other necessaries during said time; -- to send him to the night-school during the present winter -- to furnish him also at the end of his time with a suit of cloathes of the value of twenty two dollars and also with Tools to the value of Ten dollars at least.

The court adjourns until Saturday next.

Saturday 6th December 1806

At an adjourned Orphans' Court this day were present

Robert Brent, Esq., Judge -- John Hewitt, regr. of wills

Margaret Winsatt administratrix of John B. Winsatt appears and passes her first account.

Margaret Winsatt, administratrix of George Booth appears and passes her first and Final account.

Letters of administration are Granted & issued to Jekiel Crossfield, of Washington County, on the estate of Seth Carter, a lieutenant late of the Navy of the United States --

The court adjourns until Tuesday next. [page]

Tuesday, 9th December 1806

At an Orphans' Court holden in and for Washington County, at the City of Washington, on Tuesday the 9th day of December 1806 were present

Robert Brent, Esq., Judge -- John Hewitt, regr. of Wills

Ordered by consent of parties, that the hearing of the case of John and George Baltzer and others, Creditors of Charles McLaughlin decd. -- against Peggy McLaughlin his administratrix be further postponed until the First Tuesday in January next.

The court adjourns until Saturday next.

Saturday 13th December 1806

At an adjourned Orphans' Court -- were present

Robert Brent, Esq., Judge -- John Hewitt, regr. of Wills --

Ordered that David Dobbin[s], administrator of Daniel Eldridge decd. -- sell the property of the deceased at public auction first giving notice of the sale by advertisement in the National Intelligencer inserted three times And that said sale be on a credit of sixty days for all purchases exceeding Twenty dollars taking bonds or notes with security for payment with interest from the day of sale. Sales not exceeding twenty dollars to be for Cash.

Letters Testamentary are issued to Athanasius Fenwick executor of the last will and testament of James Fenwick late of Saint Mary's County in Maryland decd.

The court adjourns until Saturday next.

Saturday 20th December 1806

At an adjourned Orphans' Court, this day, were present:

Robert Brent, Esq., Judge

John Hewitt, regr. Wills

Thomas H. Gilliss, administrator of Patrick Lynch appears and passes his first account — [page]

Saturday 27 December 1806

At an Orphans' Court this day were present

Robert Brent, Esq., Judge

John Hewitt, register of Wills

James Dunlop, appears and files the following caveat:

To the Orphans' Court of Washington County in the District of Columbia

James Dunlop appears and files the following caveat against the probate, by this court, of the will of Robert Peter, deceased

To the Orphans' Court of Washington County:

As one of the representatives of Robert Peter deceased I hereby enter by Caveat against proving a certain nuncuputative [sic] will of said Robert Peter which I understand is about being exhibited for probate -- as said Peter was not of sound and disposing mind memory and understanding when made.

Letters admin. [issued] to William O'Brien on estate of James Dennis.

The Court adjourns until Saturday next.

Saturday 3rd January 1807

The Court meets present Robert Brent, Esq., Judge

John Hewitt Register of wills

Ordered, on the application of Thomas Peter for a proceeding and decision on the caveat entered by James Dunlop on the 27th of Decr. last for that purpose that Citation to proceed to the establishing his said Caveat issue for the following persons, viz: James Dunlop -- and for Elizabeth Peter [page] widow of Robert Peter, widow of Robt. Peter decd., George Peter, Thomas Peter, Robert Peter & Margaret Dick, next of [kin] and for John Weems, Eliza Hosburg and [Arnane?] French as witnesses returnable on Saturday next --

Henry Ingle -- administrator of William Smilie appears and passes his account. [page]

Saturday 10th January 1807

As a special Orphans' Court holden this day were present

Robert Brent, Esq., Judge
John Hewitt, register of Wills

On the application of Walter T. Greenfield, administrator of George Beall deceased Ordered that he sell so much of the personal property of the deceased (excepting the negroes) as will be sufficient for the payment of the debts of the deceased -- either at public or private sale and for Cash or on Credit.

Ordered on the application of Isaac Pomroy administrator of John Detterly deceased that he sell the personal property of the deceased contained in his inventory on a credit of sixty days for all sums above twenty dollars -- taking bond or note with security for payment on interest and given ten days' notice of the terms of sale.

James Dunlop appears in obedience to citation at the instance of the Executors of Robert Peter decd. -- and prays a plenary proceeding -- and time to prepare for the same.

Letters of administration are issued to Henry Dearborn on the estate of his son George R. Dearborn formerly of Washington City decd.

Saturday 17th January 1807

The Register attends and in the absence of the Judge adjourns the Court till Saturday next.

Tuesday 2 February Court meets at [Shelter] & adjourns till Friday next same place. [page]

Friday 6th February 1807

The court meets -- present Robert Brent, Esq., Judge
Jno. Hewitt, Register of Wills

James Dunlop attends in proper person and also Thomas Peter, Robt. Peter, David Peter, James Peter, & by William H. Dorsey their attorney.

And the said James Dunlop files a petition praying for further time for the examination of his witnesses to substantiate his Libel against said Thomas Peter and others.

And then the court adjourns until Tuesday next.

Tuesday 10th February 1807

The Court meets -- present Robert Brent, Esq., Judge
John Hewitt, register of Wills

James Dunlop -- appears by Philip B. Key his attorney and also Thomas Peter & others by Wm. H. Dorsey, James S. Morsell their attorneys.

The Court proceeds on the Examination of Witnesses on the petition of Thomas Peter, Robert Peter and James Peter to prove a nuncupative codicil to the will of Robert Peter deceased -- and the deposition of Doctor John Weems on behalf of said petition is taken.

Elizabeth Peter the widow of Robert Peter filed with the court her renunciation of all devises and bequests under the will and codicils of said Robert Peter -- and elects, in lieu thereof, to take her dower and distribute part of his estate -- in the following words: (here insert it).

The court then adjourns. [page]

Monday 16th February 1807

At an adjourned Orphans' Court this day: --

Isaac Gillaspey an orphan boy aged eighteen years the first day of January last is produced in court and with his own consent is placed and bound out by the court as an apprentice to Thomas Murray of the City of Washington, Cooper, to serve him until he attains the full age of twenty one years. The said Thomas Murray agrees and contracts to teach the said Isaac Gillaspey his said art or trade of a Cooper, to find and provide him sufficient meat, drink, cloathing, washing and other necessaries, to have him taught common reading, writing and arithmetic in and at the end of his time to give him a set of Tools and a new suit of cloathes worth at least thirty dollars.

John Evans aged sixteen years the eleventh day of September last, having no father living, is produced in court, and with his own consent is placed and bound out by the court as an apprentice to Thomas Murray of the City of Washington, Cooper, to serve him until he attains the full age of twenty one years. The said Thomas Murray agrees and contracts to teach the said Thomas Murray his said art or trace &c. (precisely as in the preceding).

James Dunlop and Thomas and David Peter and others by their respective attorneys appear in their respective petition & libel and by consent of parties the further proceeding in the said cause is postponed until Wednesday next -- to meet at Semmes' Tavern in Georgetown at 4 o'clock P.M.

Court adjourns. [page]

Saturday 21st March 1807

At an Orphans' Court this day were present

Robert Peter, Esq., Judge -- Jno. Hewitt, regr.

Abigail Hart, administratrix of Matthias Hart deceased appears & returns an Inventory.

Ordered that Abigail Hart administratrix of Matthias Hart decd. sell the property of the deceased contained in the inventory return'd by her or such part thereof as she may think proper -- for cash -- giving Ten days notice of the sale by advertisement.

Ordered also that she Give notice to the creditors of the deceased to exhibit their claims by advertisement inserted three times in the *National Intelligencer* --

Joseph Stretch and John Craven, Executors of John Burchan appear and pass their first account.

Letters Testamentary on the will of Caesar Lowry late of Washington County deceased are Granted to Mary Lowry the Executrix named therein.

Court adjourns until Saturday next.

Wednesday March 25th 1807

At a special Orphans' Court holden at Semmes' tavern in Georgetown, Washington County, were present Robert Peter, Esq., Judge
John Hewitt, register of Wills

Pursuant to adjournment, the Court proceeds in the examination of witnesses in the case of James Dunlop and Elizth. his wife Libellants and Thomas Peter and others respondents present both parties and their counsel.

The Deposition of Stephen B. Balch a witness summoned by the Libellants, as taken. —

The court adjourns until tomorrow at 3 o'clock P.M. to meet at the same place. [page]

Thursday 26th March 1807

The Court meets pursuant to the adjournment, present
Robt. Brent, Esq., Judge -- John Hewitt, regr. of Wills

Letters of Administration on the personal estate of Rezin Beck late of Washington County deceased are Granted to Richard Beck his brother, he having produced the renunciation of Dorcas Beck widow of the deceased, in his favour.

The Court proceeds in the Examination of Witnesses in the case of James Dunlop and wife Libellants agt. Thomas Peter and others respondents. The depositions of Mrs. Nelly Peter, of John Peter and Benjamin Stoddert, produced by the Libellants are taken -- both parties and their counsel present.

By consent of parties, further proceedings in said case are posponed [sic] until Monday the 25th of May next. --

The Court then adjourns until Saturday next.

Friday 27th March 1807. Letters of administration on the personal estate of Ozias Offutt late of Montgomery County in Maryland deceased are issued, by the Register, to James Offutt of William the administrator appointed in Montgomery County. [page]

Saturday 4th April 1807

At an adjourned Orphans' Court, present

Robert Brent, Esq., Judge
Jno. Hewitt, regr. Wills --

Ordered that Richard Beck, administrator of Rezin Beck decd. sell the personal property of the decd. at public auction, That the terms of sale be on a credit of ninety days to all purchasers above twenty dollars, taking Bonds or notes with good security bearing interest from the day of sale, all sales not exceeding twenty dollars to be for cash. He shall advertise notice of said sale in the *Washington Federalist* and *National Intelligencer*, the notice to be inserted three times in each paper, previous to the sale.

Ordered also that the said Richard Beck give notice to the Creditors of the said Rezin Beck to exhibit their claims against him, by advertisement in the usual form inserted in said papers once a week for three weeks.

George Hurley an orphan boy, aged about fifteen years as nearly as can be ascertained is bound by the court with his own & the consent of Isaac S. Middleton his brother in law, as an apprentice to John Petherbridge of the City of Washington a Shipwright to serve him for the term of five years and three months from the first of the present month of April at said trade. The said John Petherbridge agrees to take the said George Hurley as an apprentice and contracts to teach and instruct him in the said art or trade of a Shipwright in and during his said apprenticeship to find and provide for him good and sufficient meat, drink, cloathing, washing, lodging and other necessaries -- to have him instructed in common reading, writing and arithmetic -- and at the end of his time to furnish him with a good suit of cloathes worth at least twenty two dollars -- with a set of proper tools for his trade — [page]

Tuesday 14th April 1807

At an orphans' Court -- present Robt. Brent, Esq., Judge -- Jno. Hewitt, regr. of Wills.

Richard Kenney a poor boy destitute of the means of support aged seventeen years on the 17th day of August next is brought into court by John Hebron of the City of Washington, Ship Calker, and by his own consent is placed and bound out by the Court as an apprentice to the said John Hebron to serve him as such until he attain the age of twenty one years. The said John Hebron engages and agrees on his part to teach and instruct the said Richard Kenney in the said art or business of a Ship-calker in the best manner in his power -- and during his apprenticeship to find and provide for him good and sufficient meat, drink, cloathing, lodging and other necessaries -- to have him instructed in common reading, writing and arithmetic -- and at the end of his term to give him a set of working tools and a good common suit of cloaths and also a freedom suit worth at least twenty two dollars.

John Williams aged sixteen years on the 20th day of March last, a poor boy destitute of the means of support is brought into court by the revd. Francis Neale [illegible] vice-President of the George-town College, and with his own consent is placed and bound out by the court to the said Francis Neale as vice president of the Georgetown College in said

said [sic] County -- to serve as an Apprentice to the trade or business of a Taylor until he attain the age of twenty one years at said College -- And the said Francis Neale agrees to take the said John Williams under his direction and undertake to have the said apprentice well and sufficiently taught and instructed in the said art trade or business of a Taylor -- to have him provided and supplied with sufficient meat, drink, washing, cloathing, lodging and other necessaries during [page] said term -- taught reading, writing and arithmetic and provided with a good suit of cloathes at the expiration thereof --

Letters of Collection are Granted to Benson L. McCormick on the personal estate of Andrew Long late of Washington City and county deceased.

Benson L. McCormick having applied for Letters of administration on the personal estate of Andrew Long late of Washington County decd. Ordered that he give notice thereof by advertisement inserted three times in a Baltimore paper.

Saturday 18 April 1807

An adjourned Orphans' Court -- present

Robert Brent, Esq., Judge -- Jno. Hewitt, regr. Wills

Ordered that Washington Boyd and George Moore Executors of John Wrightt deceased sell such part of the personal property contained in the inventory returned by them as they may deem necessary -- for payment of debts & on such terms as may be in their opinion most advantageous --

Joseph Charles aged 17 years -- bound to John Rawlings, shoemaker -- to learn him his trade -- to teach him reading, writing and arithmetic, to find him in meat, drink, clothing & other necessaries, and to give him a set of tools & suit of cloathes worth 22 dolls. at the end of his time.

The Court adjourns untill Saturday next --

Saturday 25th April -- The Court adjourns until Saturday 9th May. [page]

Saturday 9th May 1807

At an adjourned Orphans' Court holden this day were present Robt. Brent Esq., Judge -- John Hewitt, regr. Wills --

Letters of administration are Granted to Sarah Thompson on the estate of her brother Richard Nelson late of Washington County decd.

Ordered that Ann Calvert, administratrix of Joseph Calvert decd. give Notice to Creditors to Exhibit their claims by advertisement inserted in the National Intelligencer once a week for three weeks.

Ordered also that she sell the personal estate of the decd. contained in the inventory. That the same be sold on a Credit of Three months for all sums above twenty dollars taking bonds or notes for payment with interest, Under that sum the sale shall be for cash -- But she shall previously give notice of said sale by advertisement inserted at least three times in the *National Intelligencer*.

May 14/5. Application is made by Thomas Summers for administration on the estate of Budgit Chubb a seaman decd.

Washington Boyd applies same day for letters on same estate.

Saturday 16th May 1807

At an adjourned Orphans' Court were present -- Robert Brent, Esq., Judge
John Hewitt, register of Wills

Letters of administration are granted to Washington Boyd on the estate of Budgit Chubb. [page]

Ordered that George Blagden Administrator of William Swinton give notice to creditors by advertisement inserted three weeks in the *National Intelligencer*.

The court adjourns until Saturday next.

Saturday 23 May 1807

At an adjourned Orphans' Court holden this day were present
Robert Brent, Esq., Judge
John Hewitt, register of Wills --

Ordered that Sarah Thompson administratrix of Richard Nelson decd. sell the property of the decd. contained in his Inventory for Cash -- giving notice of said sale by advertisement set up at public places in the City of Washington.

Ordered also that she give notice to Creditors to bring in their claims by advertisement inserted once a week for three weeks in the *National Intelligencer*.

Monday 25th May 1807

At an Orphans' Court holden at Semmes' Tavern in George-Town, present Robert Brent, Esq., Judge -- John Hewitt, register of wills --

Ordered that Benson L. McCormick Administrator of Andrew Long deceased sell the property of the deceased -- contained in the inventory on a credit of sixty days for all sums above five dollars taking notes or bonds with security for payment and giving ten days notice of the sale by advertisement.

Letters of Administration were Granted to Benson L. McCormick on the estate of Andrew Long of Washington County decd. [page]

Thomas Peter, Robert Peter, David, & George Peter appear by J.T. Mason and J.S. [Morsell], Esq., their Attorneys -- as also James Dunlop by P.B. Key, Esq. his Attorney -- when the court proceeds in the Examination of Witnesses on the case of Thomas Peter and others agt. James Dunlop and the Examination of Doct. John Weems on the part of the former is taken --

The Court adjourns until tomorrow morning, 10 o'clock to meet at the same place --

Tuesday 26th May 1807

The Court meets persuant to adjournment

Present Robert Brent, Esq., Judge
John Hewitt, regr. of wills --

The court proceeds in the examination of Dr. John Weems on the part of the Respondents Thomas Peter & others at suit of James Dunlop & wife.

Eliza Horsburgh a witness produced on the part of the said Respondents is also examined --

By consent of parties in said case a commission to examine further witnesses is issues [sic] to Charles Evans.

Saturday 30th of May 1807

At an adjourned Orphans' Court this day were present

Robert Brent, Esq., Judge
John Hewitt, regr. of Wills

Abner Ritchie and Charles A. Beatty administrators of Charles Beatty deceased appear and pass their 3rd and 4th accounts. [page]

Application is made by David ~~W.~~ Drane for Letters of administration on the estate of Francis Ware Tubman --

The court adjourns until Saturday next.

Saturday 6 June 1807

Insert the issue in Peter's case &c. --

Alice Dermott appears and as administratrix *cum testamento annexo* of James R. Dermott, passes her first account --

The court adjourns until Tuesday next.

Tuesday 9th June 1807 (2 Tuesday)

At an Orphans' Court holden this day, present — Robert Brent, Esq., Judge & Jno. Hewitt, Regr.

Adjourns till Saturday 20th next. [page]

Saturday 20th June 1807

At an adjourned Orphans' Court holden this day were present

Robert Brent, Esq., Judge and John Hewitt, regr. of Wills --

Janet McDonald a poor Girl, daughter of Andw. McDonald & Elleanor his wife, whose parents have forsaken her and left her and her property unprovided for and unprotected and aged between 7 and 8 years is produced in court and the court appoints Henry Tuel her Guardian.

The following petition of Thomas Peter, Robert Peter, David Peter and George Peter is presented and filed.

(Here insert it)

Whereupon the following decree was passed by the Court --

(here insert it)

The court adjourns until Saturday next.

Saturday June 27th 1807

The court meets -- present Judge and register and adjourns until Saturday the eleventh instant.

Saturday 11th July

The register in the absence of the Judge adjourns the court until Saturday the 18th instant. [page]

Saturday 18 July 1807

At an adjourned Orphans' Court this day were present Robert Brent, Esq., Judge
Jno. Hewitt - regr. Wills

Benjamin Talburtt a poor boy aged thirteen years the 18th day of September next is with his own and his mothers' consent bound by the court as an apprentice to Joseph Carberry of the City of Washington, Hatter, to serve him as an apprentice until he attain the age of twenty one years ~~as an~~ to said trade -- the said Joseph Carberry agrees to teach the said apprentice his said trade -- to provide him with sufficient meat, drink, cloathing and other necessaries -- to teach him common reading, writing, and arithmetic and at the end of his time to give him a new suit of cloaths in addition to his common apparel.

Enoch Lowe a poor boy aged 18 years the 2nd of September next, is with his own and his mother's consent bound to Joseph Carberry of the City of Washington, hatter (on the same terms as above).

Merit Taltum aged sixteen years the 20th day of December next -- a poor boy having no parent within the District of Columbia is produced in court and with his own consent is bound to said Joseph Carbery [sic] on the same terms --

The court adjourns until Saturday next. [page]

Monday 27 July 1807

At an adjourned Orphans' Court this day were present Robt. Brent, Esq., Judge
Jno. Hewitt, register of Wills

Rebecca Forrest Executrix of Uria [sic] L. Forrest decd. appear and passes her first account --

And the court adjourns until Saturday next.

Saturday 1st August 1807

At an adjourned Orphans' Court -- present

Robert Brent, Esq., Judge
Jno. Hewitt -- regr. Wills

Samuel Ritcharded [sic], an orphan boy aged fourteen years on the first day of December last as nearly as can be ascertained -- ~~an orphan boy~~ is brought into court by James Patterson of the City of Washington Boot and shoemaker -- and is bound by the court to the said James Patterson as an apprentice to said trade until he arrives at the age of twenty one years -- The said James Patterson engages and agrees to teach the said Samuel Ritchardson the said trade or art of a Boot and shoemaker -- to provide him with sufficient meat, drink, washing, lodging and other necessaries -- to have him instructed in common reading, writing, and arithmetic and, at the end of his time, to give him a new suit of cloathes worth at least 22 dollars and a set of Tools --

Ordered that George Blagden Executor of William Swinton deceased -- sell the personal property of the deceased contained in the inventory -- returned by him this day, at [page] public auction -- for cash -- giving six days notice of the sale by advertisement.

Daniel Busserd administrator of Martin Whelan appears and passes his second and final account.

Jane Baker, Executrix of Samuel Baker appears persuant to citation at the suit of George St. Clare one of her securities in the administration -- Whereupon it is Ordered that the said Jane Baker give good and sufficient counter security to be approved of by the court on or before the second Tuesday of the present month.

John Harryman Kreager -- a poor boy who is destitute of the means of support -- but whose age cannot be ascertained -- tho, apparently he is about sixteen, is brought into court by William Steuart of Georgetown in the District of Columbia -- And the said boy, with his own consent and at his own request, is placed and bound out by the court as an Apprentice to the said William Steuart, to serve him as such until he attain the full age of twenty one years. -- The said William Steuart agrees and engages that during said term he will cause the said John Harryman Kreager to be brought up to and instructed in the art or business of a Mariner or Seaman -- at which business it is understood he is to serve his apprenticesp. also that he will, during said term, find and provide for said apprentice good and sufficient meat, drink, cloathing, washing, lodging and other necessaries -- will have him instructed in common reading, writing and arithmetic -- and that, at the end of his apprenticeship he will give him a new suit of cloathes worth at least twenty two dollars —
[page]

Tuesday 11th August 1807

At an Orphans' Court holden this day were present Robert Brent, Esquire, Judge
John Hewitt -- Register of Wills --

Elias B. Caldwell administrator of Gustavus Scott appears and prays further time to settle his account of his administration which is Granted him till the second Tuesday in October next.

Solomon Stinger — administrator of John Stinger decd. appears persuant to citation and returns an Inventory.

Elizabeth Wilson administratrix of Alexander Wilson decd. appears on Citation -- Ordered that she sell the personal property contained in the inventory return'd by her -- at public auction -- That the sale be on a credit of six months on all sales exceeding twenty dollars -- taking bond or notes with Good security payable with interest -- all sales not exceeding twenty dollars to be for Cash. She shall give at least fifteen days notice of the sale by advertisement inserted three times in the *National Intelligencer.*

Rachel Murray, formerly Rachel Masters, administratrix of Richard Masters decd. appears on Citation -- Ordered that she be allowed time until Saturday next to settle the account of her administration.

James D. Barry applies for Letters of administration *de bonis non* on the estate of William Hearn of Baltimore.

Verlinda Selby Executrix of Henry Selby appears on Citation, and passes her first account. [page]

Saturday 15th August 1807

An adjourned Orphans' Court this day were present

Robert Brent, Esq., Judge
Jno. Hewitt, regr. Wills

Samuel N. Smallwood, administrator of Richard Frazer decd. appears in obedience to Citation and passes his first account account [sic].

Washington Boyd one of the administrators of Catherine Johnson decd. appears and passes their first account.

The court adjourns to Saturday next.

Saturday 22nd August 1807

At an adjourned Orphans' Court this day -- present

Robert Brent, Esq., Judge -- Jno. Hewitt, regr. wills.

Letters of administration are Granted to John K. Smith of Washington County -- a creditor, on the personal estate of Daniel Jennings late of the Navy of the United States, purser --

Ordered that he give notice to creditors to exhibit their claims by advertisement inserted three times in the *National Intelligencer* --

Alexander McCormick, administrator of John Scott deceased, appears on Citation and passes his first account.

Ordered on the application of Joseph Carleton for Letters of Administration *de bonis non cum testamento annexo* on the estate of Christopher Richmond decd. that the same be issued to him on his filed bond with approved securities with the Register of Wills --

Jno. Bridges administrator of Christian Slimmer appears on Citation -- & passes his first account.

Court adjourns until Saturday next — [page]

Saturday 29th August 1807

The Register of Wills attends and absent the Judge, adjourns the Court until Saturday next.

Saturday 5th September 1807

At an adjourned Orphans' Court present Robert Brent, Esq., Judge -- Jno. Hewitt, register of Wills --

Michael Scott -- surviving administrator of John McCarty appears and passes his First account.

John Hoye acting Executor of Francis Deakins deceased appears and passes a second account.

Rebecca Hodgson administratrix of Joseph Hodgson appears and passes a second and final account.

Ordered that Rebecca Hodgson, Guardian of [blank] Hodgson and of [blank] Hodgson infant children of Joseph Hodgson deceased apply the rents and profits of the real estate to which they are entitled towards their education and maintenance.

Letters of administration are Granted to Andrew Duncan of Boston as a creditor on the personal estate of Edward Innis late of the United States' schooner *Experiment* deceased.

Adjourns until Saturday next.

Saturday 12 September 1807

An adjourned Orphans' Court present Robert Brent, Esq., Judge -- Jno. Hewitt, regr. Wills

Richard T. Spalding son of Enoch Spalding aged nineteen years on the 5th day of November next is produced in court by his father and with his fathers and his own [page] consent is placed and bound out by the court as an apprentice to Robert Clarke of Washington City and County Painter and Gla[z]ier to serve him as such until he attains the full age of twenty one years -- And the said Robert Clark -- being in court agrees to take the said Richard T. Spalding as his apprentice -- and to teach him or cause him to be taught his said trade or art of painting and Glazing -- to find and provide him good and sufficient necessaries and support during his apprenticeship -- to give him at least two months nights schooling and at the end of his time a suit of cloathes worth twenty two dollars.

Betsy a free black girl (commonly called Betsy Wallace), aged 13 years on the first day of March last is brought into court by John Threlkeld her Guardian -- and is bound out to Robert Clarke, Sr. of Georgetown in Washington County to serve him as an apprentice until she attain the age of sixteen years -- to learn the business of a Housewife -- The said Robert Clark agrees that he will cause her to be taught the said business -- and particularly that she shall be taught common plain sewing & do ordinary house work -- and shall not be removed out of the District of Columbia -- Shall be provided her with necessary meat, drink, washing, cloathing, lodging, medicine and other necessaries -- And when free that he will give her one good warn winter suit of cloathes -- and one of Summer -- both plain --

four brown linen shifts -- a pair of shoes and stockings -- and three Blankets — [page]

Rachel Pratt -- administratrix of John W. Pratt appears and passes her First account.

Charles Glover acting administrator of John Crookshank deceased appears and passes a second account.

Adjourn until Saturday next.

Saturday 19 September 1807

The court meets

Present Robert Brent, Esq., Judge
John Hewitt -- Register Wills

Mary Bradley an poor orphan Girl aged about Ten years -- is produced in court by the revd. Mr. Neale Principal of Georgetown College and is bound out by the court to said College as an apprentice to be instructed under the direction of said Mr. Neale or his successors, in the duties & business of Housewifery & Sewing also to be taught common reading, writing and arithmetic -- Mr. Neal undertakes and promises to see the same performed. She to serve until sixteen years of age.

Adjd. [page]

Saturday 26th September 1807

At an Adjourned Orphans' Court present

Robert Brent, Esq., Judge -- Jno. Hewitt, regr. wills

Letters of Administration are Granted to Thomas Hunter on the personal estate of Samuel Whann late of Washington County deceased

Then the court adjourns until Saturday next.

Saturday 3rd October 1807

An adjourned Orphans' Court -- present

Robert Brent, Esq., Judge -- John Hewitt, regr. Wills

Henry Knowles administrator of Nathaniel Wilkins appears and passes his First account.

Adjourn'd till Saturday next.

Tuesday 13th of October 1807

At an orphans Court present Robert Brent, Esq., Judge -- Jno. Hewitt, regr. wills

Ordered that citation issue agst. Jane Burch administratrix of Jesse Burch.

Adjourned until next Saturday.

Saturday 17th of October 1807

At an adjourned Orphans' Court this day were present
Robt. Brent, Esq., Judge
Jno. Hewitt, regr. of Wills

Jane Burch administratrix of Jesse Burch appears on citation at[?] of Thomas Burch and passes her first account.

It appearing by the account of Jane Burch, administratrix of Jesse Burch deceas'd [page] passed this day that there is in her hands a balance of six hundred and two dollars and thirteen cents -- exclusive of an outstanding debt of one hundred and twenty dollars still due by the deceased -- which being deducted leaves the sum of $482.13 cents in her hands to be distributed -- Ordered that the same be distributed in manner following, viz: One third thereof namely $160.71 to be retained by herself as widow -- the remaining two thirds, viz $321.42 to be divided equally among the five children of the deceased -- amounting to the sum of $64.28½ cents each --

Joseph Milligan—administrator of John March appears and passes his first account.

Cornelia DeKraftt, admx. of Charles DeKrafft appears on citation and passes her first account.

George French -- Executor of Margaret Scott appears and returns an Inventory.

Alice Hepburn -- adminx. of David Hepburn appears and returns an Inventory.

And then the court adjourns until Saturday next.

Saturday 24th October 1807

At an adjourned Orphans' Court this day were present Robert Brent, Esq., Judge
Jno. Hewitt - register of Wills

The court adjourns until Saturday next.

Saturday 31st October 1807

The court meets and adjourns until Saturday next. [page]

Saturday November 7, 1807

The Register adjourns the court the Judge not attending until next Saturday.

Saturday Nov. 14, 1807

The court meets and adjourns -- until Saturday next.

Saturday 21 November 1807

The Register in the absence of the Judge adjourns the court until Saturday next.

Saturday 28 November 1807

At an adjourned Orphans' Court present

Robert Brent, Esquire, Judge

John Hewitt, Register of Wills

Ordered that George Kirkpatrick administrator of Samuel Kirkpatrick deceased sell the personal property of the deceased contained in the inventory at auction -- giving notice of the sale by advertisement inserted twice in the *National Intelligencer* -- And that the same be sold on a credit of sixty days on all sales exceeding Ten dollars -- taking Bonds or notes with security for payment & with interest from the day of sale -- All sales not exceeding Ten dollars for Cash.

Ordered that Nicholas Lingan and Jno. R. Magruder administrators of George Lee deceased Give notice to Creditors to Exhibit their claims by advertisement in the usual form inserted twice a week for three Successive weeks in a Georgetown and in a Baltimore newspaper.

Elias B. Caldwell administrator of Gustavus Scott deceased appears and passes his Final account.

Thomas Herty one of the administrators of James Thompson appears and passes an account. [page]

Letters Testamentary are issued to Mary McDermott Roe on the will of her husband Cornelius McDermott Roe she having entered into Bond with securities as required by law.

The court having read and considered the depositions of the witnesses to the will of Thomas Jenkins late of Washington County deceased as taken by the register of Wills on the 23rd instant and considering that this court exercise Jurisdiction, in matters Testamentary, over personal property only -- It is adjudged and decreed that the said probate is sufficient to authorize the issuing of Letters Testamentary on the said will and that the same be accordingly issue to Francis Jenkins the Executor therein name[d] --

The court adjourns until Saturday next.

Saturday 5th December 1807

The Register adjourns the court in the absence of the Judge until Tuesday next the court in course.

Tuesday 2nd in December (8th day) 1807

At an Orphans' Court this day were present

Robert Brent, Esq., Judge -- Jno. Hewitt, Regr. Wills

Ann Hurdle, Executrix of Leonard Hurdle appears on Citation and passes her first account.

Summons having heretofore issued for Kinsey Gittings one of the securities of Jane Burch administratrix of Jesse Burch deceased to answer the petition of Thomas Burch which having been served on him by the Marshall and he having failed to appear, Ordered that an Attachment issue against him. [page]

Letters of administration are Granted to William Prince of Washington County on the personal estate of Joseph Ferguson late of the United States frigate *President* ordinary seaman decd.

Letters of administration are Granted to William Prince of Washington County on the personal estate of John Jobs late of the United States frigate *Constitution* deceased.

Court adjourns until Saturday next. [page]

9th January 1808

At an Orphans' Court this day were present Robert Brent, Esq., Judge -- John Hewitt, register of Wills

William Hurley an orphan boy aged seventeen years and three months on the second instant as nearly as can be ascertained is brought before the court by George McCaulley of the City of Washington Boat-builder -- and with his own consent and the consent of his brother in law Isaac J. Middleton is placed and bound out by the court as an apprentice to the said George McCaulley to serve him as such until he attain the full age of twenty one years -- The said George McCaulley on his part agrees to take the said William Hurley as his apprentice and contracts and engages to teach and instruct or cause to be taught and instructed the same William Hurley the said art or business of Boatbuilding -- to find and provide for him sufficient meat, drink, cloathing, washing and lodging and other necessaries fit for an apprentice and to send him to nights school every winter during his apprenticeship --

William Rogers an orphan boy aged sixteen years on the second day of February next is brought before the court by George McCaulley of the City of Washington Boat-builder and with his own consent is placed and bound by the court as an apprentice to the said George McCaulley to serve him as such until the full age of twenty one years. The said George McCaulley on his part agrees to take the said William Rodgers as an apprentice -- and contracts and engages to teach and instruct or cause to be taught and instructed the said William Rodgers the said art or business of Boatbuilding -- to find and provide for him sufficient meat, drink, cloathing, washing and lodging and other necessaries fit for an apprentice and to send him to night's school every winter during his apprenticeship — [page]

Ordered on application and by consent of Parties that a cause between the State of Maryland use of Levin Campbell agst. Elias B. Caldwell administrator of Gustavus Scott deceased be referred to Benjamin Stoddert —

Same orders in the case of State of Maryland use of Ann Campbell same use of Isabella Campbell and same use of Hardy & wife agst. said E.B. Caldwell administrator of Gusts. Scott.

On the application of Nicholas Lingan one of the Executors of George Lee deceased, praying for further time to return a list of debts due the said deceased, Ordered that the said Executor be allowed the further time of two months from the 1st instant for that purpose —

Saturday 30th January 1808

Present Robert Brent, Esq., Judge
Jno. Hewitt, regr. Wills.

Charles Snell aged sixteen years on the twelfth day of December last poor boy destitute of the means of support whose parents reside out the District of Columbia is produced in court by William Stoops of Georgetown -- ship carpenter -- and with his own consent the said Charles Snell is placed and bound out by the court as an apprentice to the said William Stoops, to serve him at the said business of a ship carpenter until he attain the age of twenty one years. The said William Stoops on his part agrees to teach the said apprentice his said Trade or business of a ship carpenter -- to find and provide for him sufficient meat, drink, washing, cloathing, lodging and other necessaries, during his apprenticeship -- to give him three winters' nights schooling and at the end of his time to give him a set of Journeyman's Tools and a good new suit of cloaths --

Ordered that John McGowan and Michael Nourse Executors of Geo. Mitchel sell the personal property contained in the Inventory on a credit of three months on all sales above twenty dollars -- taking note or bond for payment on int. & giving 10 days notice of sale. [page]

Saturday 6th February 1808

At an adjourned Orphans' Court this day present
Robert Brent, Esq., Judge -- Jno. Hewitt, Regr. Wills
The court adjourns until Tuesday next.

Tuesday 9th February 1808

At an Orphans' Court on the second Tuesday of February 1808 --
present Robert Brent, Esq., Judge
John Hewitt, Register of Wills

Ordered that Kinsey Gittings, one of the securities of Jane Burch, admx. of Jesse Burch, sell the negroes belonging to the estate of the deceased which have come into his possession by order of this court -- for the purpose of distributing the money arising therefrom among the representatives -- and that the same be sold on a credit of 6 months taking Bond with security on Interest & giving reasonable notice of such sale.

William Prince administrator of James Lovell appears and passes his account.

Gerard Gibson admr. of Jane Kissick appears & passes his account.

Lewin Talburtt, administrator of James Robinson appears & passes his acct.

Adjourned until Saturday next.

Saturday 13th February 1808

An adjourned Orphans' Court
Present Robt. Brent, Esq., Judge, Jno. Hewitt, Regr.

Orlando Cook, admr. of Francis McClure appears & passes his final account.

Ordered that Christina Hamilton admx. of Saml. Hamilton sell so much of the property contained in the Inventory as will pay his debts -- credit 6 months on all sums above 20 dollars 15 days notice.

Ordered that Washington Boyd & Geo: Moore Exors. of John Wright sell as above.

Adjourn until Saturday next. [page]

Saturday 20 February 1808

The Register in absence of the Judge adjourns the court until Saturday next.

Saturday 27th February 1808

The court meets -- present Robt. Brent, Esq., Judge
John Hewitt, Register of Wills

Leonard H. Johns one of the Executors of Elisha O. Williams appears and passes his first account.

Court adjourns until Saturday next.

Saturday 5th March 1808

Court meet -- present Robt. Brent, Esq., Judge
Jno. Hewitt, Regr.

Christina Hamilton administratrix of Samuel Hamilton appears and passes her first account.

Court adjourns until Saturday next.

Saturday 12th March 1808

The court meets -- present Robt. Brent, Esq., Judge
Jno. Hewitt, regr. Wills

Adjourns until Saturday next.

Saturday 19 March 1808

The court meats and adjourns until Saturday next.

Saturday 26th March 1808

The court meets pursuant to adjournment
present Robert Brent, Esq., Judge
Jno. Hewitt, Regr. of Wills --

John Tanner a poor boy whose mother is living in Virginia aged sixteen years on the 27th day of February last is brought into court by Thomas Williams of the City of Washington, Blacksmith, and with his own consent & the application and consent of his mother Mary Tanner, signified in writing & filed is bound by the [page] Court as an apprentice to said Thomas Williams to learn his said Trade -- and to serve until he attain the age of Twenty one years -- And the said Thomas Williams hereby agrees and engages to teach the said John Tanner his art or business of a Blacksmith -- to find and provide him sufficient meal, drink, washing, cloathing and lodging during his apprenticeship -- to give him at least six months schooling and at the end of his time a good new suit of cloathes worth at least twenty two Dollars.

Letters of Administration are issued to Marianne C. Murdock and George French on the personal estate of Addison Murdock late of Washington County decd.

Ordered that Marianne Murdock & George French Administrators of Addison Murdock Give notice of their administrations and for Creditors to exhibit their claims by Advertisement in the usual form, inserted in the *National Intelligencer* and *Washington Federalist* once a week for three weeks.

Gustavus M. Ware an Orphan appears in Court and being of lawful age to make choice of a Guardian -- prays that Charles A. Burnett of Georgetown in Washington County may be appointed by the Court -- and the said Charles A. Burnett being present in court is accordingly appointed Guardian of the person and property of the said Gustavus M. Ware, he having entered in Bond with approved security for the performance of his duty as required by Law.

Abner Ritchie and Charles A. Beatty, administrators of Charles Beatty appear & pass their 5th account.

Adjourn'd till Saturday next.

Saturday 2 April 1808

The Register of Wills in the absence of the Judge adjourns the Court further until Saturday next. [page]

Tuesday 12th April 1808

At an Orphans' Court holden the second Tuesday in April 1808 were present

Robert Brent, Esq., Judge
Jno. Hewitt, Regr. Wills

Richard Beck, administrator for Rezin Beck deceased appear and passes his first account.

Charles A. Burnett, Guardian of Gustavus M. Ware having returned an Inventory of personal property belonging to said Ware -- and pray'd that he may be empowered to sell the same in order to vest the proceeds in Bank or other stock -- and it appearing to the court that it will be most beneficial to the said minor to do so -- The same is Ordered accordingly.

Ordered that Marianne C. Murdock and George French Administrators of Addison Murdock deceased sell the personal property of the deceased contained in the inventory returned by them, this day or so much thereof as they may deem necessary -- on a credit of six months for all sales above twenty dollars -- and giving at least five days' notice of the Sale in the *Washington Federalist* and *National Intelligencer* -- and taking bond with security for payment with interest -- all sums not exceeding twenty dollars to be for Cash --

Adjourned until Saturday next.

Saturday 16th April 1808

At an adjourned Orphans' Court this day -- present

Robert Brent, Esq., Judge -- Jno. Hewitt, Regr. Wills

Ordered that Rachel Keefer and Thomas Hyde Administrators of Henry Keefer deceased to give notice to the Creditors of the deceased -- to exhibit their claims by advertisement in the usual form, inserted for three weeks in the *Washington Federalist* --

Ordered also that they sell the personal property contained in the inventory return'd by them -- at Public auction for Cash -- & that they give at least Ten days' notice of the sale by advertisement inserted twice in said paper — [page]

Mrs. Jane Burch brings into Court her four children Thomas Burch aged about eighteen years, Kilty now in her fourteenth year -- Jesse aged Ten years and Fielder aged twelve years and is appointed Guardian of their person and property.

She enters into Bond with George St. [Clare] as her Security for the performance of her duty --

It appearing by an order of distribution made by the court on the 17th of October last that each of the above mentioned children is entitled to the sum of 64 dollars 28½ cents as their distributive share of their deceased father Jesse Burch -- And it appearing also that the said Jane Burch has been burthened with the maintenance and education of them since the decease of their said father now near five years -- Ordered that the said maintenance and education be allowed and considered as payment in full of their said shares.

Adjourned.

Tuesday 19th of April 1808

The court meets at the request of John G. Jackson, Letters Testamentary are issued to John G. Jackson one of the Executors of Mary Payne late of Washington County deceased -- Washington Boyd the other named Executor having renounced.

Letters of administration are issued to Thomas Rigden on the personal estate of Thomas Rigden late of Washington County deceased -- Lucy Rigden widow and John E. Rigden eldest son of the deceased having renounced in his favour.

Adjourned. [page]

Saturday 23 April 1808

At an adjourned Orphans' Court present --

Robt. Brent, Esq., Judge

Jno. Hewitt, regr. Wills --

Ordered that the Executrixes of John Beckley deceased, sell the goods and chattels of the deceased contained in the inventory return'd by them. That said sale be on a credit of six months for all sums exceeding twenty dollars -- for other sums on a credit of thirty days, taking bonds or notes with good security, bearing interest from the day of sale.

Fifteen days' notice of the sale to be given by advertisement inserted in the *National Intelligencer*.

Adjourn'd.

Tuesday 26th April 1808

John Davidson one of the Executors of Joseph Taylor appears and passes his account.

Adjourn'd until Saturday next.

Saturday 30 April 1808

Meets and adjourned until Thursday next. [page]

Thursday 5th May 1808

At an adjourned Orphans' Court -- present

Robert Brent, Esq., Judge -- Jno. Hewitt, regr.

Thomas Dant an orphan boy who was here before (viz on the 4th of September 1802) bound by the court to the revd. Leonard Neale President of the Georgetown College -- appears in court with said Neale and with his own consent and at his request and by mutual agreement -- the said contract is rescinded and the said Thomas Dant is now bound out & placed as an apprentice to Thomas C. Wrightt of Georgetown merchant taylor -- to serve him untill he attain the age of twenty one years. The said Thomas C. Wrightt hereby engages and contracts to have the said Thomas Dant instructed in said trade of a Taylor and to find and provide him, during his apprenticeship, sufficient meat, drink, cloathing, washing & lodging -- to have him taught common reading, writing and arithmetic and at the end of his time to give him a new suit of cloathes.

Adjourn'd until Sat'y. next.

Saturday 7th May 1808

At an adjourn'd Orphan's Court present

Robert Brent, Esq., Judge -- Jno. Hewitt, Regr. Wills

Ordered that the Executors of George Mitchell give notice for Creditors of the deceased to exhibit their claims by advertisemt. inserted 6 times in the *National Intelligencer*.

Adjd. [page]

Saturday 14th May 1808

The Register adjourns the court in the absence of the Judge until Saturday next.

Saturday 21st May 1808

At an adjourned Orphans' Court this day
present Robert Brent, Esq., Judge
Jno. Hewitt, Regr. Wills

Ordered that Daniel Brent Administrator of Edward [Killen] deceased give notice for Creditors to exhibit their claims against the deceased by advertisement in the usual form inserted once a week in the *National Intelligencer.*

The court adjourns until Saturday next.

Saturday 28th May 1808

The court meets present Robert Brent, Esq., Judge
John Hewitt, Regr.

George Washington Brooke a poor boy aged ~~fourteen years~~ who was born on the 14th of September 1794 is bound apprentice to John Minchin Boot and Shoemaker on the usual terms &c.

Adjourn'd. [page]

At an adjourned Orphans' Court This 4th June 1808
Present Robert Brent, Esq., Judge
Jno. Hewitt, regr.

Susanna Daugherty an orphan born the second day of September in the year 1798 is brought into court by her uncle Joseph Daugherty and with the consent of her said uncle she is placed out and bound as an apprentice to Patrick Deery of the City of Washington -- to serve him as such until she attain the full age of sixteen to learn Housewifery & sewing. The said Patrick Deery engages and contracts that he will have her instructed in Housewifery & sewing -- that he will find and provide for her sufficient meat, drink, washing, cloathing and lodging and other necessaries during said term -- have her taught reading and writing -- & at the end of her time will furnish her with a new suit of cloaths.

Thomas B. Beall one of the Executors of George Beall decd. appears and passes his first account.

Christina Hamilton administx. of Samuel Hamilton appears and passes her second account.

George Blagden Executor of William Swinton decd. appears and passes his first & final account.

Adjourns until Saturday next.

Saturday 11th June 1808

William Rhodes having this day applied for Letters of admn. on the personal estate of Henry Kramer &c. decd. Ordered that he give notice thereof by advertisement inserted once a week for six weeks in the Natl. Intel-- one paper publishd. on the eastern shore & one in the city of N. York. [page]

Tuesday 14 June 1808

At an Orphans' Court holden on the second Tuesday being the 14th day of the month of June 1808 -- present Robert Brent, Esq., Judge, John Hewitt, Register. The court adjourns until Saturday the second of July next.

Saturday 2nd July 1808

An adjourned Orphans' Court is holden this day -- present Judge Brent and the Register -- & the same is further adjourned until Tuesday next.

Saturday 9th July 1808

At an adjourned Orphans' Court present

Robert Brent, Esq., Judge

John Hewitt, regr. Wills

Ordered that Thomas Rigden Administrator of Thomas Rigden give notice to Creditors of the deceased to exhibit their claims, by advertisement in the usual form inserted once a week for three weeks in the *Washington Federalist*.

Ordered further that he sell the personal property of the deceased -- contained in the inventory returned by him on a credit of ~~six~~ three months to all purchasers above the sum of thirty dollars -- taking bonds or notes with good security for payment with interest from the day of sale -- Sales not exceeding ~~twent~~ 30 dollars to be for Cash -- He shall give notice of the sale by advertisement inserted at least twice in the *Washington Federalist*.

Joseph Stretch and John Craven Executors of John Burchan appear & pass their 2nd account.

Adjd. till Saturday. [page]

Saturday 16th July 1808

At an adjourned Orphans' Court -- present Robert Brent, Esquire, Judge -- Jno. Hewitt, Register of Wills

Adjourned until Saturday next.

Saturday 23rd July 1808

The Court meets and adjourns until Saturday next.

Saturday 30th July 1808

The court meets --

Thomas H. Gilliss Executor of Stanley Byus appears and passes his first account.

Adj. till Saturday next.

August 4, 1808

Letters Testamentary issued by the Register to Mary [Mitchell] Executrix of John Mitchell of Washington County deceased.

By order of the Judge in writing Letters of administration are issued to William Rhodes on the personal estate of Henry Kramer deceased.

Saturday 6th August 1808

The court meets, present Robert Brent, Esq., Judge
Jno. Hewitt, Regr.

Ordered that William Rhodes administrator of Henry Kramer decd. give notice for the creditors of the deceased to exhibit their claims against him by advertisement in the usual form inserted three weeks in the *National Intelligencer.*

Ordered also that the said William Rhodes sell the goods and chattels of the decd. contained in the inventory filed -- on a credit of sixty days for all sums above twenty dollars -- taking bonds or notes with security for payment on interest from the day of sale -- other sales to be for Cash. Notice of the sale to be given by advertisement inserted twice in the *National Intelligencer.* [page]

Tuesday 9 August 1808

The Judge not attending the Register adjourn'd the court till tomorrow.

Wednesday 10 August 1808

The Court meets.

John Hoye administrator *de bonis non* of William Deakins appears and passes his first account.

John Hoye one of the Executors of Francis Deakins appears and passes his Third account.

Samuel Brooke, administrator of James Paxton passes his final account.

Daniel Rapine administrator of Susanna Osborn appears and passes his First account.

James Davidson Jr. administrator of James Miller passes his account.

Joseph Millegan administrator of John March appears and passes his second and final account.

William O'Brien administrator of James Dennis appears and passes an account in full.

Letters of administration are Granted to Robert Clarke on the personal estate of Isaac Wayne of Washington County decd.

Adjd.

Saturday 13 August 1808

At an adjourned court present Robt. Brent, Esq., Judge
Jno. Hewitt, Register --

James Offutt of William, administrator of Ozias Offutt of Montgomery County, Md., appears and passes his account.

Eleanor Curran, one of the administrators of John Curran decd., appears and passes her final account.

Ordered that Robert Clarke administrator of Isaac Wayne decd. give notice for creditors of the deceased to exhibit their claims by advertisement in the usual form, inserted once a week for three weeks in the *Washington Federalist*.

Ordered also that the said administrator sell the personal property contained in the inventory returned by him, on such terms as he may [page] deem most beneficial -- giving at least seven days notice of the sale by advertisement in the said paper.

The will of Nicholas Mitchell late of Washington County decd. is proved specially to notice and Letters Testamentary thereon are Granted to Gustavus Howard the Executor therein named.

Adjd.

Saturday 20 August 1808

At an adjourned Orphans' Court this day present
Robert Brent, Esq., Judge -- Jno. Hewitt, Regr.

James Lowry of Washington County, aged fourteen years on the 25th day of July 1808, the infant son and one of the Legatees and devisees of Caesar Lowry decd. is brought into Court and the said James Lowry makes choice of Mary Lowry his mother to be the Guardian of his person and property -- which choice is approved of and confirmed by the court -- and the said Mary Lowry enters into Bond in the penalty of Five thousand dollars with Nicholas Hodges and James Moore as her sureties for the faithful performance of her duties as Guardian.

George Lowry of Washington County aged Ten years on the ninth day of July 1808, the infant son and one of the Legatees and devisees of Caesar Lowry decd. is brought into Court -- and the court constitutes and appoints Mary Lowry his mother to be the Guardian of his person and estate -- the said Mary Lowry enters into Bond in the penalty of Two thousand dollars with Nicholas Hodges and James Moore as her sureties, for the faithful performance of her duties as Guardian --

Rebecca Lowry of Washington County who will be seven years of age on the ninth day of October 1808, the infant daughter and one of the Legatees and devisees of Caesar Lowry deceased is brought into Court and the court constitutes and appoints Mary Lowry her mother to be the Guardian of her person and property. The said Mary Lowry enters into Bond in the penalty of two thousand dollars with Nicholas Hodges and James Moore as her sureties, for the faithful performance of her duty --

Adjourn'd until Saturday next. [page]

Saturday 27th August 1808

The register in the absence of the Judge adjourns the court until Saturday next.

Saturday 3rd September 1808

At an adjourned Orphans Court present

Robert Brent, Esq., Judge -- Jno. Hewitt, Regr.

The court having ordered that Letters of administration on the personal estate of William Hearn late of Baltimore deceased ~~and that the~~ be granted to James D. Barry and that the caveat filed by Johanna Barry against issuing the same ~~be dismissed~~ and her application for Letters be dismissed.

Ordered that Mary Mitchell Executrix of Capt. John Mitchell decd. give notice to the Creditors of the deceased to exhibit their claims by advertisement inserted once a week for 3 weeks in the *Washington Federalist* and the same number of times in the *National Intelligencer*.

Adjourned to Saturday next.

Saturday 10 September 1808

At an adjourned Orphans' Court this day present

Robert Brent, Esquire, Judge
Jno. Hewitt, Register

There being no business -- the Court is further adjourned until Saturday next.

[end of record]

Index

Heritage Books by Wesley E. Pippenger:

Alexandria (Arlington) County, Virginia Death Records, 1853–1896

Alexandria City and Arlington County, Virginia Records Index: Vol. 1

Alexandria City and Arlington County, Virginia Records Index: Vol. 2

Alexandria County, Virginia Marriage Records, 1853–1895

Alexandria Virginia Marriage Index, January 10, 1893 to August 31, 1905

Alexandria, Virginia Marriages, 1870–1892

Alexandria, Virginia Town Lots, 1749–1801
Together with the Proceedings of the Board of Trustees, 1749–1780

Alexandria, Virginia Wills, Administrations and Guardianships, 1786–1800

Alexandria, Virginia 1808 Census (Wards 1, 2, 3, and 4)

Alexandria, Virginia Death Records, 1863–1896

Alexandria, Virginia Hustings Court Orders, Volume 1, 1780–1787

Connections and Separations: Divorce, Name Change and Other Genealogical Tidbits from the Acts of the Virginia General Assembly

Daily National Intelligencer *Index to Deaths, 1855–1870*

Daily National Intelligencer, *Washington, District of Columbia Marriages and Deaths Notices (January 1, 1851 to December 30, 1854)*

Dead People on the Move: Reconstruction of the Georgetown Presbyterian Burying Ground, Holmead's (Western) Burying Ground, and Other Removals in the District of Columbia

Death Notices from Richmond, Virginia Newspapers, 1841–1853

District of Columbia Ancestors,
A Guide to Records of the District of Columbia

District of Columbia Death Records: August 1, 1874–July 31, 1879

District of Columbia Foreign Deaths, 1888–1923

District of Columbia Guardianship Index, 1802–1928

District of Columbia Interments (Index to Deaths)
January 1, 1855 to July 31, 1874

District of Columbia Marriage Licenses, Register 1: 1811–1858

District of Columbia Marriage Licenses, Register 2: 1858–1870

District of Columbia Marriage Records Index
June 28, 1877 to October 19, 1885: Marriage Record Books 11 to 20
Wesley E. Pippenger and Dorothy S. Provine

District of Columbia Marriage Records Index
October 20, 1885 to January 20, 1892: Marriage Record Books 21 to 30

District of Columbia Marriage Records Index
January 20, 1892 to August 30, 1896: Marriage Record Books 31 to 40

District of Columbia Marriage Records Index
August 31, 1896 to December 17, 1900: Marriage Record Books 41 to 65

District of Columbia Probate Records, 1801–1852

District of Columbia: Original Land Owners, 1791–1800

Early Church Records of Alexandria City and Fairfax County, Virginia

Georgetown, District of Columbia 1850 Federal Population Census (Schedule I) and 1853 Directory of Residents of Georgetown

Georgetown, District of Columbia Marriage and Death Notices, 1801–1838

Husbands and Wives Associated with Early Alexandria, Virginia (and the Surrounding Area), 3rd Edition, Revised

Index to District of Columbia Estates, 1801–1929

Index to District of Columbia Land Records, 1792–1817

Index to Virginia Estates, 1800–1865
Volumes 4, 5 and 6

John Alexander, a Northern Neck Proprietor, His Family, Friends and Kin

Legislative Petitions of Alexandria, 1778–1861

Pippenger and Pittenger Families

Proceedings of the Orphan's Court, Washington County, District of Columbia, 1801–1808

The Georgetown Courier *Marriage and Death Notices:*
Georgetown, District of Columbia, November 18, 1865 to May 6, 1876

The Georgetown Directory for the Year 1830: to which is appended, a Short Description of the Churches, Public Institutions, and the Original Charter of Georgetown, and Extracts of the Laws Pertaining to the Chesapeake and Ohio Canal Company

The Virginia Gazette and Alexandria Advertiser:
Volume 1, September 3, 1789 to November 11, 1790

The Virginia Journal and Alexandria Advertiser:
Volume I (February 5, 1784 to January 27, 1785)

Volume II (February 3, 1785 to January 26, 1786)

Volume III (March 2, 1786 to January 25, 1787)

Volume IV (February 8, 1787 to May 21, 1789)

The Washington and Georgetown Directory of 1853

Tombstone Inscriptions of Alexandria, Volumes 1–4

Made in the USA
Coppell, TX
24 March 2026

74575411R00057